Edinburgh

D0544604

A guide to recent architecture

• • •

Johnny Rodger
Photographs by John Niall McLean

Edinburgh

A guide to recent architecture

● ● ● ellipsis

BRITISH LIBRARY CATALOGUING IN PUBLICATION
A CIP record for this book is available from the British Library

Edinburgh: a guide to recent architecture

PUBLISHED BY •••ellipsis
2 Rufus Street London N1 6PE
E MAIL ...@ellipsis.co.uk
WWW http://www.ellipsis.com
SERIES EDITOR Tom Neville
EDITOR Rosa Ainley

COPYRIGHT © 2001 Ellipsis London Limited
ISBN 1 84166 066 3

PRINTING AND BINDING Hong Kong

•••ellipsis is a trademark of Ellipsis
London Limited

For a copy of the Ellipsis catalogue or
information on special quantity orders
of Ellipsis books please contact
us on 020 7739 3157 or sales@ellipsis.co.uk

Johnny Rodger 2001

Contents

The Renaissance of Edinburgh: Das Kapital

In the new millennium the visitor to Edinburgh arriving at the airport and penetrating the city thence, west to east, might find their attention held not by the distant profile of the Castle Rock or Arthur's Seat but by the procession of building works and new construction that lines their route. The visitor passes by the Gyle Centre and Edinburgh Park (see page 11.6), the new Murrayfield Stadium, and the new Millennium Green housing at Slateford (page 9.14) is not far off their route to the south. They pass the Morrison Link hotels (page 9.6); the new financial centre, the Exchange with its conference centre (page 5.4); the giant glass crescent of Scottish Widows (page 5.24); they travel on through the Grassmarket. Just off the axis is the new Museum of Scotland (page 7.2) and then the Festival Theatre. New housing lines the way and they come to Holyrood North with its bars, cafés, restaurants, hotels and its poetry library; on the other side of the road is The Scotsman Building (page 3.4), and Dynamic Earth (page 3.2). Finally the long road culminates not at Holyrood Palace, but at the new Scottish Parliament (page 2.38).

From airport to parliament is or ought to be a more significant modern journey than from castle to palace. Is this then the Democratic League rather than the Royal Mile? The enlightened visitor might indeed feel entitled to assume that a reinvigorated civic and democratic spirit put about by the existence of the new parliament had spurred the citizens to these constructive exertions. Indeed, writer Alasdair Gray's personal motto – 'Work as if you were in the early days of a better nation' – has a certain resonance here.

But with what accuracy could the visitor make such an assumption about the impetus behind all this new building work? It is not only on this corridor – south-east to west – but all over the city, in every other area from Wester Hailes to Leith, that a mass of new construction has taken place since the early 1990s. But the fact is that most of it was already planned and much of it completed before the people of the country had even elected to have their own parliament (in late 1997), far less had decided (or rather, been told) where to site the building.

Other factors more mundane than the urgings of the 'democratic spirit' can explain this spate of new building. But it might be helpful to look briefly at history in order to understand why so much new building was thought necessary, and how it was possible in the middle of a very old city.

By the 1500s the Old Town of Edinburgh, sited on the escarpment of the Castle Rock, was already an established royal European capital, but in successive centuries it lost its royalty (1603, to London), its parliament (1707, to London), and its ruling and upper classes (the last society ball was held in the Old Town in 1817). It is often said that Edinburgh's greatest glory, the Scottish Enlightenment period of the late eighteenth and early nineteenth centuries which produced the likes of David Hume and Adam Smith, was possible only once its royalty and parliament were lost because then such intellects could discourse free from the squabbling of ruling-class party politics that had dogged Scottish history.

In the Old Town people had lived at a density of up to 700 per acre; the mixing of people of different classes, trades and temperaments was therefore unavoidable and this undoubtedly contributed to great debate and cross-fertilisation of ideas once political squabbles were out of the way. The building of the Georgian New Town, however, intended ostensibly as a handsome attempt to attract aristocrats back from London, ensured that nobody had to meet people from another class or, in fact, anybody at all on those wide streets unless they so wished. Neither was there to be any of the bustle or the industry of the Old Town. As Youngson points out in his book *The Making of Classical Edinburgh*, the inhabitants of the New Town were swift to invoke planning regulations or to go to law to prevent the intrusion of its by-products – noise, smell, etc. – into the 'genteel and well ordered arcady' of the New Town.

The historian Owen Dudley Edwards has made the case that the last victim of Burke and Hare, who murdered 16 people in 1828 and sold their bodies for dissection, was the Scottish Enlightenment itself. Nor is it only a metaphorical case, for the discovery of their grisly murders led to changes in the law which stifled the supply of bodies to the anatomy and medicine departments of the university and thus excluded the possibility of real experiment in the one field of inquiry still vibrant at that time in the city.

Subsequently – and conforming to a somewhat orthodox Marxist interpretation of history – the economic truth behind this parade of human misery came out when five years after the Burke and Hare murders, with a change of town council, the city was found to be bankrupt. It had spent too much and overborrowed to pay for the building of the New Town. The Enlightenment was well and truly finished as Burke and Hare were revealed as extreme representatives of an isolated and resentful underclass abandoned on the penniless rock of the Old Town by their benighted so-called betters.

Edinburgh did not then so much go into decline as slumber; it was no longer the capital of an independent country, it was no longer renowned for its intellectual status as the Athens of the North; it was a provincial backwater having, as Charles McKean put it, 'a post-New Town siesta'. It continued thus right up until the 1970s when the Old Town population fell as low as 1500 people. Edinburgh was nonetheless a much changed city by this time. In addition to the New Town were great areas of Victorian suburbs like Gorgie, Dalry and Comely Bank, genteel middle-class garden suburbs of villas and terraces like Corstorphine, Trinity and Braids, and much of the lost population of the Old Town had been decanted out to peripheral council estates like Wester Hailes and Craigmillar. With this physical spread the city had entered into a period which can fairly be described as a love-affair with the motor car.

Edinburgh displayed classic symptoms of love-sickness: neglect, self-loathing and, ultimately, self-mutilation. The loved one was to be given licence to roam and a new inner-city ring road was planned. This meant demolishing buildings, tearing gaps in the city fabric and generally blighting such areas as Greenside, the Pleasance, Nicolson Street/South Clerk Street, Tollcross and the former Caledonian Railway Station at Lothian Road. Then in 1984 a Labour administration took over from the Conservatives, and brought a whole new dynamic. It seems incredible now to think that up until that date the city had no development agency.

The inner-ring-road proposals were abandoned and the Lothian Region Structure Plan of 1985 stimulated activity both in the blighted zones listed above and in other brownfield sites throughout the city. Planning and economic studies indicated that if the city were to flourish, it would have to consolidate in certain sectors – principally in financial services, but also in hotel accommodation and conference facilities.

In the financial sector it was clear that larger open-plan buildings with deeper floorplates to cater for the new technologies and systems of administration were needed. The Georgian and Victorian buildings of the traditional 'golden rectangle' of the financial sector of the city between St Andrew's and Charlotte Squares were no longer suitable.

Regretably, in order to promote regeneration of these city-centre sites in accordance with their planning and economic studies, the council chose not to organise open competitions among architects for the design of masterplans (the traditional and successful method for design of the New Town). Instead they held a series of developer competitions for such sites as the Caledonian Railway Station, the Morrison Street Goods Yard (see page 9.2), and Holyrood North (see page 2.2). While this might mean that the vision, aesthetic and general motive may be compromised by some short-term commercial ethic, there does exist a record of more or less successful examples of such public/private partnerships – all the more commendable given that much of the programme was undertaken during a period of general economic recession.

One notable exception to the developer-led competition is the Edinburgh Park business development (see pages 11.6–11.10). Much has been made of comparisons and similarities between the Edinburgh Park masterplan and James Craig's plan for the first New Town. But the fact is that the award of the commission for the design of this site was even further from the open, principled and democratic procedure of New Town planning than those commercial competitions listed above inasmuch as the council went directly to a world-famous American modernist architect – Richard Meier – and asked him to come up with a masterplan.

Despite these cavils about the commissioning, the park has, by the developer's own standards, been quite a success. The original intention was to attract major corporate headquarters to a site between the city and the airport that would provide spacious and light modern offices in a pleasant landscaped environment that was, nonetheless, urban in character rather than being a part of the suburban sprawl. The success is clear to see: all the completed buildings are occupied.

Yet the siting of the park does seem to involve the council in a certain contradiction of both its own policies and of the general trend in urban development. The tenets of Richard Rogers' 'urban renaissance' and both Edinburgh City Council's stated aim to reduce car use and promote public transport in the city and their actual measures of green routes, bus lanes and road closures seem to have been forgotten here. The council has set a target to reduce the proportion of people who travel by car in the city from 48 per cent in 1991 to 34 per cent in 2002 and Councillor David Begg said their transport strategy was aimed to ensure 'maximising accessibility rather than movement *per se*'. But this type of site on the remote edge of town – and other similarly placed ones like the new Royal Infirmary at Little France, and the retail parks at Straiton, Kinnaird Park, and South Gyle – is not easily accessible by public transport and so encourages car use.

Edinburgh Park defends its position by saying that soon the express rail bus system (CERT – City of Edinburgh Rapid Transport) will pass through on its way to the airport and in addition to that a new railway station is being built. But why then, you might wonder, all the on-site parking spaces? Besides, these answers do not address the criticism that these developments put pressure on Edinburgh's green belt, and only make it more difficult for the council to protect it when individual developments have already been established.

The yardstick against which the success of the plans for these big city developments (such as Edinburgh Park, The Exchange, Morrison Goods Yard) is measured is often that of the New Town plans. Perhaps it is hoped that by employing similar neo-classical geometry in the masterplan some of the New Town's grandeur and beauty will rub off, but at any rate this model is not the only one that has been employed.

Indeed, as part of the new pedestrian- and tourist-friendly city, the ecosystem of the herringbone pattern of closes (where no car may pass) leading off the High Street of the Old Town has been 'rediscovered'. In the 1990s £1.8 million was spent to reopen 26 closes, and the Holyrood North site is a larger-scale project to recreate the tight urban atmosphere on the site of the former Holyrood Brewery off the Canongate (see page 2.2). The building of housing on that site and many others led by 2000 to a gradual increase of the population of the Old Town to around 9000.

There has also been much demolition work (18 high-rise blocks have been brought down) and £60 million has been spent on housing, leisure and recreation facilities in Wester Hailes (see page 10.8). While there are still many problems associated with poverty and deprivation, a 44 per cent decrease in reported crime has been quoted. In Craigmillar a similar much-needed regeneration programme is under way, while in Leith regeneration has already begun with the siting of the new Scottish Office and the royal yacht 'Brittania' as a tourist attraction docked in front of the planned new shopping centre on the Western Harbour. Much upmarket housing has been built – notably on Rennie's Isle – and bars and restaurants have opened up. While high rises have been coming down elsewhere, there are plans to build some 20-storey ones here on the waterfront.

New housing has also sprung up on many brownfield sites throughout the city. Much of it has been built quickly and in such instantly recognisable pastiche styles as neo-vernacular, neo-Ramsay Gardens, neo-nineteenth-century tenement, neo-New Town Georgian, etc., and it is therefore not of much architectural interest. Examples of this can be seen on the former brewery site between Dalry Road and Haymarket station, on the former railway land on the other side of the station, and on the ex-industrial land at the bottom of Macdonald Road.

When our hypothetical visitors take a longer and wider look around this city they will be astonished at the amount of building that has taken place over these last ten years, and perhaps also aghast at how little it all has to do with the new 'democratic spirit'. Sure, we have a new parliamentary democracy after a gap of 300 years and the parliament building itself might be one of the jewels in Edinburgh's crown, but most of the other construction was either on the drawing board or on site before anyone knew the parliament was coming.

Can Edinburgh now say it is, politically speaking, an important European capital again? No. One famous Scottish stage personality has entertained us with his jibes at Scotland's 'pretendy parliament'. There might be more alliteration than accuracy in that quip, but nonetheless the major design and development decisions in the city over the period covered in this publication have been made by what Charles McKean has called 'secret confabulations between council committees and remote and anonymous financiers'.

Yet these 'secret confabulations' have managed to manoeuvre Edinburgh into a position where it is said to be the fourth-biggest financial centre in Europe. Is it not more likely that it is this success that has underwritten the major building work in the city, and not some Johnny-come-lately 'democratic spirit'? This book is a guide to Edinburgh's new built environment and it examines how we can read or refute the above history in the architectural design of the period.

ACKNOWLEDGEMENTS
Special thanks to Charles McKean, Eilidh Donaldson, all staff at RIAS, Ian Wall, John C Hope, Charles Prosser, and all architects involved.
JR April 2001

Edinburgh: a guide to recent architecture

How to use this book

The centre of the city of Edinburgh is split into two main parts, the Old Town, site of the original medieval city, and the New Town built in the eighteenth and nineteenth centuries.

The Old Town is built on a volcanic rock with the castle at the summit and the main thoroughfare running east–west down the escarpment towards the sea. The most dense collection of buildings featured in this book is situated here. The New Town is built on the broader, flatter hill on the other side of the Princes Street Gardens and slopes away to the north and the Firth of Forth.

Both these areas – the Old Town with its narrow alleyways (called 'closes' or 'wynds' here) and the New Town with its broad, mainly Georgian terraces – are relatively compact and easy and pleasant to walk in. Other parts of the city included here – suburbs and public-housing schemes added and villages incorporated all around Edinburgh since the Victorian age – are perhaps best reached by bus.

Lothian Buses is the largest city-wide bus company (its buses are maroon and white) and the closest bus route to each building is listed here. Most services go along Princes Street; each stop gives a list of buses stopping there and a route plan. For further transport advice Lothian Buses' information office is situated on Waverly Bridge, right next to the main rail station. You can also call Traveline (at 1 Cockburn Street) for details of all public transport on 0131 225 3858, Monday to Friday, 8.30–20.00.

Note that Lothian Buses do not give change when you purchase a ticket on board, so you must provide the exact fare (quoted on route plans at bus stops) if you don't wish to lose out.

A new light-rail bus is to be built – delayed by planning objections and a public enquiry – and will run from the airport through Edinburgh Park to the city centre and perhaps down to Leith.

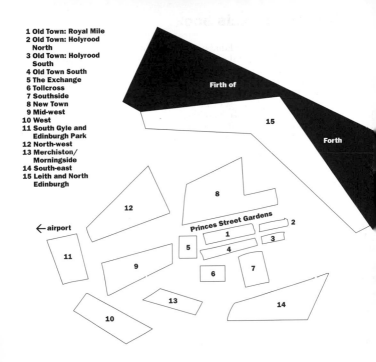

1 Old Town: Royal Mile
2 Old Town: Holyrood North
3 Old Town: Holyrood South
4 Old Town South
5 The Exchange
6 Tollcross
7 Southside
8 New Town
9 Mid-west
10 West
11 South Gyle and Edinburgh Park
12 North-west
13 Merchiston/ Morningside
14 South-east
15 Leith and North Edinburgh

Firth of

Forth

15

← airport

Princes Street Gardens

2
1
3
5
4
6
7
8
9
11
12
13
10
14

Old Town: Royal Mile

High Street Refurbishment

At one time, there were, it is said, around 600 closes leading off the Royal Mile. By the beginning of the year 2000 they numbered 83, many of them having been reopened and restored over the last ten years or so. In 1995–96 the High Street itself was refurbished by Page & Park Architects; they narrowed the highway for vehicles, thus creating broader pavements slabbed with Caithness stone, and simplified the clutter of street furniture.

They also redesigned Hunter Square with a raised plinth, which can act as an open-air performance area during the festival, over the toilets, granite benches and bronze sculptures of baskets of fruit (reminding us that this was the site of the Tron, the place where weights and measures were made). These baskets were designed by the poet Ian Hamilton Finlay and are accompanied by literary quotes and brusque Johnsonian definitions which are pregnant almost to the point of esotericism (e.g. pear – n. a paradigm of limit). To the west side of the Tron Kirk is the curvilinear organic form of a black granite sculpture, *Body and Soul* by Peter Randall-Page.

Meanwhile farther up the High Street on the north side, at the junction with George IV Bridge is a new sculpture of Hume by Alexander Stoddart. Is this Hume the Greek, as he imagined himself to be, discoursing on philosophy in his 'Enquiry', or has he just stepped out of the bath? At any rate it is a rather lean, well-toned Hume we see here with none of the Billy Bunteresque features of the contemporary portrait by Ramsay.

ADDRESS High Street
CLIENT City of Edinburgh Council
LANDSCAPE ARCHITECT Ian White Associates
CONTRACT VALUE £4.5 million
ACCESS open

Page & Park Architects 1996

Old Town: Royal Mile

Page & Park Architects 1996

Mills Mount Restaurant

Conversion of an eighteenth-century shed originally built just after the Jacobite Rising to store bread carts. Since then the building has performed many functions such as barracks, powder magazine, army stores, visitor toilets and gift shop.

The 200-seat restaurant has a timber floor and panelled ceiling and the architects' intention to build in 'traditional materials and forms with modern detailing' can be seen even from Princes Street. That northern elevation with its strip of glazing under the eaves and the vertical emphasis of its oriel/dormer windows does change the profile of the castle – but not unpleasantly.

ADDRESS The Castle
CLIENT Historic Scotland
CONTRACT VALUE £900,000
ACCESS open

RMJM Scotland Ltd 1992

Mills Mount Restaurant

Old Town: Royal Mile

RMJM Scotland Ltd 1992

The Hub (formerly Highland Tolbooth Church)

The greatest arts festival in the world, The Edinburgh Festival now has a permanent home for the first time. Offices, club/concert hall, café, bar, shop and booking facilities have all been created out of original spaces by Gillespie Graham and Pugin (1839–44), empty since the early 1980s.

The immediate impression is of colour, very bright colour. The ground-floor café is lurid yellow. (The mobile ticket stalls with roller screens designed by VK&C Design are smart and clever but only clutter this space.) The walls of the stairway at the end of the entrance corridor are painted crimson with small 'sculptured' figures by Jill Watson, said to represent various festival performances. The club room is also bright, predominantly blue, the vaulted ceiling ribs picked out in red, green, yellow or blue. The designs appear to be modelled on some painted gothic church interior, perhaps St Martin in Buda. The offices are above the roof space on adapted trusses. The deep blue of the struts is more austere here with their high-tech form contrasting with the white rendered walls.

Most people passing through this space during festival evenings will probably be going up to the Tattoo on the Castle Esplanade. So one recalls the words of Hugh MacDiarmid on that event – 'an annual atrocity perpetrated by an army of occupation upon a population of sheep. Tasteless sheep'. With its walls awash with glaring colours, perhaps this building ought to be renamed The Dip. The Sheep Dip.

ADDRESS Castlehill
CLIENT Edinburgh Festival Centre Ltd
ENGINEERS Elliot & Co
CONTRACT VALUE £7.5 million
ACCESS open, except offices

Benjamin Tindall Architects 1999

The Hub (formerly Highland Tolbooth Church)

Benjamin Tindall Architects 1999

Fishmarket Close Housing

The architects won this brief in a design competition in 1998. Two free-standing, traditional-style tall narrow buildings (7 metres wide) are to be sited with their gables facing up the close to the High Street.

Under the steep pitched roofs will be double-height maisonettes ('roofed rooms') panelled with boards of cedar. Exposed steelwork, balustrades and trims also at high level will be galvanised and unpainted. The walls are to be rendered smooth white and there will be a narrow close between the buildings.

ADDRESS Fishmarket Close
CLIENT The Burrell Company

Richard Murphy Architects 2001

Richard Murphy Architects 2001

Tron Square Nursery

Allan Murray Architects came second in the competition for the housing on page 1.8 and instead of housing get to do some child's play. A stepped wall down the east side of Old Assembly Close will mark the boundary of a two-storey building and also act as a screen providing privacy and security for the courtyard play area.

ADDRESS Tron Square
CONTRACT VALUE £500,000

Allan Murray Architects 2001

Allan Murray Architects 2001

Ibis Hotel

New build on a gap site and restoration of a category 'B'-listed building dating from 1790. The brief was to provide a 100-bedroom hotel and redevelop an existing public house on the site. The new ashlar-fronted building has an arcaded channelled stone ground floor, and eaves height to match its neighbours, plus a fifth-floor row of clerestorey windows under an oversailing roof. Something about the geometry of the arcading, the inset windows there – perhaps imitating the window high in the pediment of its neighbour – is not quite right, or are they just appropriately askew for the Old Town?

ADDRESS Hunter Square
CLIENT Accor (UK) Ltd
ACCESS open for bookings

Crerar and Partners 1998

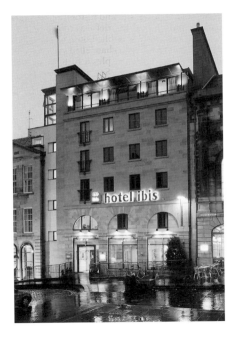

Old Town: Royal Mile

Crerar and Partners 1998

Pizza Express

The main concern for the architects on this busy thoroughfare was with volume and clarity. Internal partitions and suspended ceilings were removed. Windows to the rear were unblocked, allowing views over the rooftops, and a fully glazed frontage installed. Deep in the space an oak plane is suspended from the ceiling to conceal services and lead further into the building. Serving spaces have been removed and a dumb waiter is now used.

ADDRESS North Bridge
CLIENT Pizza Express Ltd
SIZE 375 square metres (4000 square metres)
ACCESS open to public

Malcolm Fraser Architects 1999

Malcolm Fraser Architects 1999

Fruitmarket Gallery

Remodelling the gallery involved giving it a butterfly roof, reworking the façade and moving the café and bookshop to the front of the building. The new roof flies over the old parapet level and so increases the hanging height of the upper gallery. Through the clerestorey windows thus created and the new rooflights are dramatic city views. To appreciate how this roof has opened up the building, view from the North Bridge and compare the dull flat efforts of its neighbours in the same terrace.

A galvanised-steel stairway to the first floor with an attached system of balances and weights can be easily raised by one person. This is typical of the hands-on ethos which Murphy's design encourages in the curators.

The façade has been transformed by giving it a more welcoming and rhythmic layering of materials – stone, glass, metal – and also to let in more light along the ground floor. Some of the stone façade was removed and the existing upper-floor windows closed off with lead panelling. The café and the bookshop thus seem completely open to the street – unfortunately their relationship to the gallery is not quite as clear.

The full-length window upstairs serves as a balcony and also frames the hoist which has become emblematic of this building. Perhaps smart form overrides function here – rather than place the hoist on the façade and risk ruining the exterior layering, the architect has placed it inside the window where, with a lower clearance height from the floor, it is effectively unusable. Staff invariably employ a forklift truck instead.

ADDRESS Market Street
CLIENT the board of the Fruitmarket Gallery
ENGINEER Fairhursts
CONTRACT VALUE £327,000
ACCESS open

Richard Murphy Architects 1993

Fruitmarket Gallery

Richard Murphy Architects 1993

Old Town: Holyrood North

Holyrood North Site

This area to the east of Bakehouse Close and stretching between the Canongate and Holyrood Road was the site of Holyrood Brewery. Scottish & Newcastle donated the site to The Dynamic Earth charity which was set up to run the centre of that name, situated to the south on the other side of Holyrood Road (see page 3.2).

Sensitive to the historic character of the surrounding area and aware of the work done elsewhere along the Royal Mile to restore the medieval townscape, the plan aims to reintroduce the herringbone pattern of narrow closes leading south to north off the Canongate. The developer divided the 5-acre site into 18 separate plots to be sold off for a mixed-use development of residential, retail, office and hotel accommodation. Sale of the plots helped to fund the building of The Dynamic Earth centre.

The road landscaping and the closes are to be of setts and Caithness slabbing, and it is hoped that the variety of different architects involved in this small area will give it that tight piecemeal ambience of the Old Town. 'That's exactly what the Old Town's like when you look at it', says the developer. 'It's different styles cheek by jowl'.

The attention given to this site suddenly became more concentrated, or you might even say frenzied, when in early 1998 it was announced that the new Scottish Parliament was to be built in Holyrood, just to the east. Since then the emphasis of the construction has shifted slightly towards more office and hotel accommodation and also towards the provision of more restaurants and bars.

BUS 24, 25, 35

John C Hope (masterplanner) 1992–

John C Hope (masterplanner) 1992–

Royal Fine Art Commission

A major part of Richard Murphy's work in Edinburgh has consisted of what he calls 'building inside buildings'. While he claims many different influences and sources of inspiration, here the most obvious one is Carlo Scarpa, the great Venetian post-war architect who arguably had his greatest success with 'interventions' in existing buildings. Murphy has been a careful student of Scarpa. He has published two scholarly texts on Scarpa's work and also made a film about him (with Murray Grigor). The influence is borne out in the attention to craftmanship of materials and the layering of these materials, not only in this building but also in the Royal Terrace Mews (see page 8.16), the Fruitmarket Gallery (see page 1.16), and Maggie's Centre (see page 12.16).

This sandstone building was built in the eighteenth century and was originally the laboratory and warehouse for a brewery. Murphy brings to bear the full vocabulary that he has developed for dealing with this sort of project through his studies and interventions in the buildings named above. This includes such typical features as layering of metal, wood, and stone; making unexpected openings; using sliding panels and doors (such as the sliding security grill on the large front window); using stepped partitions on the stairway; inserting a full-length ridge rooflight with triangular mirrors on the interior gables; and south-facing triangular metal balconies. These features not only create adaptable, light and dynamic spaces but also reveal layers of planar construction (like the bottom of the staircase landing window hanging down below the front door opening).

It is important for such a building that this operation works in a way opposed to 'conservation' inasmuch as it doesn't seal the building up against time but rather opens the layers of history to be seen clearly. One potential problem here is that the architect has to be continually on guard

Richard Murphy Architects 1997

Richard Murphy Architects 1997

and must remember that this vocabulary, these techniques should be applied analytically and never just perfunctorily. Otherwise we end up not with dynamic space and light but simply the Murphy Mews Kit. The ridge rooflight in the upper-floor boardroom is an example of this problem. While this feature has been successful in other buildings, the enclosed space of this room and the existence of only two relatively small windows has meant that the room overheats in summer. This inconvenience has now been partially dealt with by applying mirrored film to the outside of the glass.

ADDRESS Bakehouse Close
CLIENT Royal Fine Art Commission for Scotland
CONTRACT VALUE £265,000
ACCESS by appointment only

Richard Murphy Architects 1997

Richard Murphy Architects 1997

Wilson Court Housing

Eighteen flats of varying size and plan, one part of this scheme provides a four-storey infill on the Canongate, a cream-yellow rendered block with a café on the ground floor, six flats above and a timbered version of galleries on the top floor. The other part of the building through the pend recreates the old close that ultimately runs down across bridges past Morgan Court and out to Holyrood Road. The scale switches to a more vertical orientation in the courtyard, with a top-lit stairwell rendered in red and a hybrid of neo-Scots vernacular with top wooden galleries and gables, and 1930s nautical with metal bridges, blue corner balconies, corner windows and a curved prow to the south.

ADDRESS 138 Canongate
CLIENT Old Town Housing Association
CONTRACT VALUE £700,000
ACCESS view from exterior; café open to public

Campbell & Arnott Architects 1997

Wilson Court Housing

Old Town: Holyrood North

Campbell & Arnott Architects 1997

Crichton House

The aim of the redevelopment of this brick five-storey former brewery building was not fixed until the siting of the new parliament was decided. Residential, retail and commercial were all mooted, but with the coming of the parliament it was clear there would be a great need for office space.

The architects say that the 'qualities of the existing building are maintained and enhanced' by their design. These enhancements will come from the new north–south corridor running through the internal angle of the L-shaped building to the raised deck between E & F McLachlan's buildings to the south (see page 2.12); from the glazed screens inserted into the ground-floor openings; and the curving canopy to the new entrance in Crichton's Close.

Circulation in the building will make use of an existing hoist structure, and the robust timber trusses of the roof structure are to be maintained and exposed in parts of the top floor.

ADDRESS Crichton's Close
CLIENT Manor Properties
ACCESS view from exterior

Ungless and Latimer 2000

Old Town: Holyrood North

Cooper's Court Housing

This housing for rent extends an existing brick brewhouse on the site with old and new forming an 'island' in the centre of the whole development.

The scheme represents a victory of practical architectural good sense over dogmatic planning. In order to get the planning go-ahead, the architects were asked to make several changes to their scheme, namely not to use brick, or at least to have the brick surfaces rendered to make them blend more easily with the Old Town surroundings; to have more of a vertical orientation in the windows, especially those metal-encased ones on the west side; and to design a roof with a steeper pitch.

The architects responded to these guidelines by pointing out that the use of brick is not such a glaring *faux pas* here, firstly because the building is not on the street frontage of the Canongate and so is less likely to spoil any bearded conservationists' squinty view from their gunloop, and secondly because brick is already the most common environmental material here among the brewery buildings of the backlands. As to the question of the windows and roof, the point is that some of the sizes are building-trade standards, and it is necessary to use them to keep the cost of rented-house construction low.

The building soars up to a five-storey height including the semi-subterranean car parks. The iron grills on the car-park windows echo the almost sculptural effect of the grilled openings on the stairway at the back of the tenement on the corner of the Canongate and Crichton's Close.

ADDRESS Cooper's Court/Gentle's Entry
CLIENT Old Town Housing Association
CONTRACT VALUE £760,000
ACCESS view from exterior

E & F McLachlan, Architects 2000

Old Town: Holyrood North

E & F McLachlan, Architects 2000

Canongate Housing

Has Richard Murphy gone soft?, we ask ourselves. With this block of nine flats in the Canongate, the architect once famous for his uncompromising ways gives us timber-galleried windows, an arcaded ground floor and a motto above the door. He even popped up in a local newspaper to say, 'When I see old prints of these medieval buildings which have disappeared it makes me want to cry' (*Evening News*, 25 November 1999).

A closer look at Murphy's oeuvre tells us that he has long studied the problem of 'how historic land subdivisions had worked their way into the form of buildings where "roofed rooms" are expressed against the skyline'. Clearly his interest in the old or traditional is informed by the structure and the realities of life that produced them. His original design did have a flat-roofed terrace, and the pitched roof and timber of the galleries were only added after planning-department objections. He turned around the restriction of pitched roofs by creating triangular clerestories filling in the roofline and patent glazed rooflights.

The lower floors are rendered blockwork and in the beam over the colonnade in the ground floor is the punning sinuous metalwork of an impersonalised paraphrasis of the envoi from James Joyce's *Portrait of the Artist*. It reads 'a nation is forged in the hearth of poetry' and was created by artist John Creed. The last two words turn the corner into Crichton's Close and so lead us aptly, together with the stepped back plan of the housing, into the internal square with the Poetry Library on the left.

ADDRESS 112 Canongate
CLIENT Old Town Housing Association
ENGINEERS Wren & Bell
CONTRACT VALUE £370,000
ACCESS view from exterior

Richard Murphy Architects 1999

Canongate Housing

Old Town: Holyrood North

Richard Murphy Architects 1999

Scottish Poetry Library

The Scottish Poetry Library moves half a mile eastward from Tweedale Court to a new building off the Canongate; the seat of Scottish government moves 400 miles north to be its near neighbour. How wonderfully significant it might seem to future historians. Yet it is mere coincidence – albeit laden with irony. For, as Tom Leonard once asserted, 'poets are the unacknowledged thingwaybobs'.

But Malcolm Fraser doesn't let the power of 'poetry' go to his head: this is a sturdy, modern, practical, painted, steel-frame building infilled with glass and sliding oak panels. It is on three levels with a stainless-steel monopitch roof overhanging a courtyard and front stair on which open-air readings can be held. Yet a certain gradual absorption of history and poetic effect are experienced by users of this building.

There are also subtle references to the traditional metaphor of writing and letters as trees, and the library as a forest. The Caithness stone in the courtyard is carved with oak leaves (by sculptor Mary Bourne), the perforated *brise-soleil* dapples the oak panelling with sunshine, and inside the light from the clerestorey windows and the circular rooflights plays on the faint green of the walls.

Built on a sixteenth-century gable and the remains of a seventeenth-century city wall, both the mudstone front forestair and the south-facing wooden oriel reproduce vernacular forms. At the same time the stair serves as auditorium seating for readings from the granite lectern at the front door.

Underneath the stairs set into the blue-glazed brick wall are the wooden garage doors, again of oak panelling. This garage houses the library's outreach van. In the oak-furnished interior the circulation is around the central stairway which leads either up to the mezzanine landing or down to the basement storage area. This circular movement – up, for example,

Malcolm Fraser Architects 1999

Old Town: Holyrood North

Malcolm Fraser Architects 1999

to the mezzanine, through the members' room out on to the balcony, and again back down through the auditorium to the front door – creates a spiralling sensation. Could it perhaps be a dramatic representation of the ancient cup and ring carvings in Argyll?

The feeling, at any rate, is of a quiet dynamism. As Fraser says, the library 'is not a repository – it is a resource for the revitalisation of Scottish culture'.

ADDRESS Crichton's Close
CLIENT Scottish Poetry Library
ENGINEER Elliot & Co.
CONTRACT VALUE £560,000
ACCESS open

Malcolm Fraser Architects 1999

Old Town: Holyrood North

Malcolm Fraser Architects 1999

The Tun

A mixed-use development, Allan Murray Architects' design won first place in an invited competition. The former brewery 'tun' is being transformed into housing, offices and retail units with a 'signature' building, clad in copper, zinc and glass, added to the south gable as a 'stop' to Holyrood Road.

A new concrete frame is to be inserted into the original tun building which will support slab floors with exposed concrete soffits, and two new floors, with a gallery. An attic, fully glazed on the east and west elevations, will be added.

The new-build addition will also be of concrete-frame construction. Behind the canted glass façade is a café-bar (on ground and mezzanine), office space, and a rooftop restaurant overlooking the Crags. This building, with its shops, offices, restaurants and bars, is set to be something of a bustling social centre in Holyrood. Recognition of this role and of its closeness to the new parliament comes from the BBC which is to take office space here and close its Queen Street offices.

It is unfortunate that the floors added to this building steal some of the light and panorama from the Poetry Library, but the library is a small building deep into the site – if, like Goethe, you want 'mair licht', then the oldest lesson of the Old Town is reach for the sky.

ADDRESS Jackson's Entry/Holyrood Road
CLIENT Whiteburn Holyrood Ltd
ENGINEERS Ove Arup & Partners
CONTRACT VALUE £5.4 million

Allan Murray Architects 2001

Allan Murray Architects 2001

Morgan Court Housing

In order to meet the brief (for 91 study bedrooms in 24 flats and a general store) and maintain the north–south orientation of entrances up to the Old Town, Ungless and Latimer opted for two separate blocks of housing above a raised courtyard entrance which is the roof over the shop.

The base of the buildings and practically the whole of the tower front elevation of the most easterly building are faced in Fyfestone with bands of blue brick which give it a textured geological feel. This is appropriate not just because the buildings face up to the Salisbury Crags (behind Lochview Court) but also because this site is right beside the historic edge of the Old Town city wall.

The irregular heights and patterns of this stone, along with the coloured walls above – like the wet-dash harl to the west – give the building that homely historico-geological aspect without making it simply pastiche. In the oddly unrushed and spacious shop the steel-framed structure gives the clear spans required while the residences have load-bearing structure for the main part, though in places it is supported by the frame. The roof reproduces the traditional pitch of the Old Town but is made of aluminium. All the other external metalwork, like the bridges joining the buildings (and giving an extra social aspect over the courtyard), the balustrading, and bin and bicycle store below the raised Slater's Steps, has been galvanised for low maintenance.

ADDRESS Holyrood Road
CLIENT Hart Builders (Moray House)
ENGINEER Harley Haddow Partnership
ACCESS view from exterior; supermarket open to public

Ungless and Latimer 1998

Old Town: Holyrood North

Ungless and Latimer 1998

Hammermen's Entry Housing

These 24 houses for rent for Lothian Housing Association form a U-shape, opening to the south with a raised courtyard on a grey reconstituted-stone plinth. The houses themselves are very reminiscent of 1970s-style council flats and, as *Building Design* said, are a 'disappointing take on the vernacular'. Grim and rather drab, even the coloured walls look cheap and rushed, finished on one plane only as they are, instead of wrapped around corners like the colours on Morgan Court (see page 2.22) across the way. One almost incredible fact is that the dreary grey stone of the plinth to this building was more expensive than the Fyfestone facing of the lower floors of Morgan Court.

ADDRESS Hammermen's Entry/Slater's Steps
CLIENT Lothian Housing Association
ACCESS view from exterior

Van Heyningen & Haward 1998

Hammermen's Entry Housing

Old Town: Holyrood North

Van Heyningen & Haward 1998

Holyrood Road/Slater's Steps Housing

These six- and seven-storey blocks, which mirror the plan of Morgan Court (see page 2.22) and on the east side look over the garden and restaurant on Gentle's Entry, provide 36 houses, shops and parking on the ground floor. At first-floor level they face workshops above the cycle sheds along Slater's Steps. Extensive glazing on the top level allows for views of the Crags, but otherwise these blocks are somewhat heavy and have nothing of the playfulness or delight in form, colour and material that we see in Morgan Court.

ADDRESS Holyrood Road/Slater's Steps/Gentle's Entry
CLIENT Elphinstone Homes
ACCESS view from exterior

Hackland and Dore/Gilbert Associates 1999

Hackland and Dore/Gilbert Associates 1999

Apartment Hotel

This seven-storey, 42-unit apartment hotel was built from new on the site of the demolished brewery. The concern on this cramped site – as with much of the new construction in Holyrood North – is one of scale. John C Hope, the masterplanner, had encouraged the use of coloured render in the buildings, so here colour and different geometric configurations have been used in an attempt to break up the massing and to help us read the building.

The white wall with horizontal bands of stone leads the eye up Gentle's Entry from Holyrood Road to where the dark blue of the double gable provides a stop. Round the corner, the red tower with curved metal roof gives a landmark finish to the building.

ADDRESS Gentle's Entry
CLIENT Hotel Connections
CONTRACT VALUE £2.4 million
ACCESS open for bookings

Walter Wood Associates 1999

Apartment Hotel

Old Town: Holyrood North

Walter Wood Associates 1999

Jackson House

This four-storey, round-ended gushet building (or gusset; one which goes round a corner) houses shop space on the ground floor and offices on the upper floors. With its pastiche of galleried windows on the west, a small terrace on its back, and dormers and barrel-vaulted eaves adding interest to the eastern roofscape, the architect is attempting here an ironic playfulness with traditional forms, heightened somewhat by the cladding in standing-seam stainless steel. The intention, however, is not only to contrast the contemporary and the traditional but, with use of material (such as the stone base and the steel cladding), to bring into play paradigms from the natural and both the man-made geometric and more pragmatic environments.

ADDRESS Gentle's Entry/Jackson's Entry
CLIENT Manor Properties
ENGINEER Harley Haddow
CONTRACT VALUE £1.02 million

John C Hope 2001

Jackson House

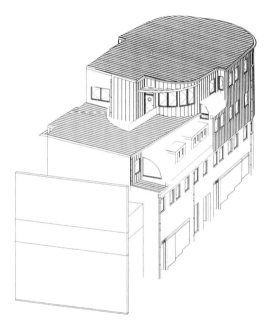

John C Hope 2001

Clocktower

The rubble infill of the south-facing arch of this former brewery building is to be removed and replaced with planar glass. The clock will be refurbished and repositioned on this glazed front. Structural supports are set back from the glazed front elevation and clad in aluminium.

As the public areas of this building are to be centred around the south (clock) and west (to Gentle's Entry) elevations, on the east and north existing windows are to be infilled with matching brick. The windows to Gentle's Entry are sandblasted glass with aluminium frames.

Of the three floors, two are taken up with the main restaurant/bar area with kitchen and toilet facilities to the rear, and the third, smaller floor has an office, toilet and plant. The upper restaurant floor has a balustraded curved edge over the void to the glass front. In front of the building a channel of water in a sandstone culvert runs down towards Holyrood Road to a coloured uplit helicoidal sculpted sandstone fountain with slots cut around the top edge through which the water pours. This feature centres the whole Holyrood North site with water, colour, light and movement.

ADDRESS 111 Holyrood Road
CLIENT Scottish & Newcastle Retail Ltd

Thompson McLeod Associates 2001

Thompson McLeod Associates 2001

Macdonald Hotel

This eight-storey hotel was partly redesigned and upgraded to include additional bedrooms and facilities – conference and function facilities, a restaurant, bars, swimming pool, gymnasium, and leisure and beauty clubs – when the parliament site next-door-but-one was announced.

A coursed sandstone double-height plinth with the upper building rendered in cream yellow, all public spaces are to the front of the building with views of the crags. Supposed to mimic the narrow frontage of the Old Town buildings, the gable is in fact split by a glazed feature, and it is difficult to see how, with too many buildings of this bulk, the area will be able to continue as a World Heritage rather than a Disney site.

ADDRESS Holyrood Road
CLIENTS Holyrood Hotels Ltd
ACCESS open for bookings

Hendry & Legge 1999

Macdonald Hotel

Old Town: Holyrood North

Hendry & Legge 1999

Holyrood Road Apartments

A massive seven-storey U-shaped block of flats opening on to Holyrood Road is set between the Macdonald Hotel and the parliament. The central gardens will be controlled by a concierge. A commercial unit will stand on either side and a clocktower on the axis.

Eighty-two apartments are to be built on a scale which will match those on either side, and there will be ground-floor parking. Traditional materials like sandstone and render will be used, while the penthouses will be cedar-clad with gullwing roofs.

ADDRESS Holyrood Road
CLIENT Teague Homes

Campbell & Arnott Architects 2001

Campbell & Arnott Architects 2001

Scottish Parliament

The architects Enric Miralles Benedetta Tagliabue with RMJM Scotland were selected to design the parliament in a competition which was described by one Scottish architect as 'a travesty, done in too much of a rush' (*Evening News*, 11 December 1999). It is further alleged by some that there was an element of undeclared interest on the panel of judges. Nonetheless it must be said that of all the entrants to the competition this design was not only the most sensitive to the site, but also the most original, contemporary and yet careful with the historic resonance – Queensberry House and the Palace – of Holyrood.

The parliament occupies the whole site at the bottom of Holyrood Road and the Canongate, although the most popular site to house it would have been on Calton Hill. The assembly building comprises a series of oval or elliptical volumes with squared-off ends containing committee and meeting rooms, ministerial and support functions, a press building and the debating chamber. The debating chamber has seating ranged around the speaker in a horseshoe form and has a press and public gallery at each side. The oval or elliptical shapes were said to be originally inspired by upturned boats the architect saw on a beach (not in Scotland, but Northumbria).

To the west there is an office building running north to south designed on a regular square grid which will cater for MSPs and their staff. Queensberry House, a grade A-listed building on site, was central to Miralles' plans at first, but after some suggestions that it might in fact be cleared from the site, they have decided to keep it after all, for modern office use, refitting the interior, knocking down some walls, removing some parts of the viewing tower and, some say, pantiling the roof – quite unsuitable for such a grand building.

A thick buff sandstone wall – The Constituency Wall – up to 5 metres

Enric Miralles Benedetta Tagliabue with RMJM Scotland Ltd 2002

Enric Miralles Benedetta Tagliabue with RMJM Scotland Ltd 2002

thick and inspired by Scottish castles, runs down the side of the Canongate, adorned with the symbols of each constituency in the country and topped by a private rooftop garden.

One criticism of the plans is that these buildings will simply not be big enough for their functions. In the debating chamber, for example, there will only be 170 places in the public gallery – fewer than half the number in the temporary parliament at The Mound. Another, purely design, concern is that while Miralles seemed at first with his upturned rowing boats to have understood something of the Old Town fishbone pattern of streets and closes, these volumes appear to have rotated in the development of the project, and now point more or less upwards to the Castle.

These days the media seem to see it as their part in the construction of public buildings – be it the Parliament, the new Royal Infirmary, or the Museum of Scotland – to whip up a furore among their readers. To this end they adopt that well-known outraged tone of thin-lipped parsimony and add the mean, uninformed jibes that pass for architectural criticism. The case of the new Scottish Parliament is no different: on the parsimony front they are claiming it as an outrage that a building which was originally costed at £40 million excluding VAT and fees, then raised to £62 million, which meant a gross total of £109 million, finally had a £195 million ceiling imposed on it in April 2000. No attempt is made, however, to establish just how expensive it is in comparison with other similar buildings here or elsewhere. As for the jibes, Miralles' boat and horseshoe shapes have been compared to bananas, coffins and boomerangs, and a touch of xenophobia was admixed with the 'criticism' when the MSP building was described as looking like an 'el cheapo hotel'.

The early and sudden death of Miralles from a brain tumour in July 2000 caused further crises for this project. The Scottish Executive's chief

Enric Miralles Benedetta Tagliabue with RMJM Scotland Ltd 2002

architect said that Miralles' 'major contribution as a conceptual architect' had already been completed and that his Scottish partners, the firm RMJM, had 'fleshed out in detail' his ideas. Some architects have reacted angrily to this 'rewriting history' and suggest that since Miralles is no longer involved 'the flare and sparkle has gone' (*The Architects' Journal*, 6 July 2000). *The Architects' Journal* ran a website poll on 13 July 2000 with the question, 'Will the eventual Scottish Parliament be a fitting testimonial to Miralles?'. Sixty-eight per cent of voters answered in the affirmative.

ADDRESS Holyrood
BUS 24, 25, 35

Enric Miralles Benedetta Tagliabue with RMJM Scotland Ltd 2002

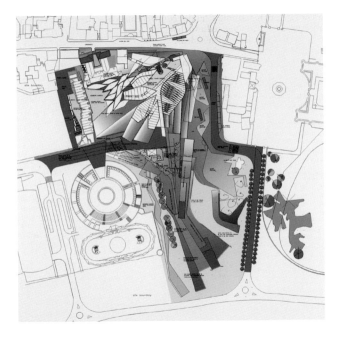

Enric Miralles Benedetta Tagliabue with RMJM Scotland Ltd 2002

Old Town: Holyrood South

The Dynamic Earth

What exactly is The Dynamic Earth? To look beyond the cosmic truism of the name and attempt even a superficial architectonic description (supposing such a thing to be possible) of this phenomenon doesn't seem to clarify the issue. A low, broad, stone amphitheatre operates as a gate and stairway to a large tented structure mounted on a plinth, half of whose load-bearing masonry walls once supported a Victorian brewery.

Inside the plinth itself, an interactive series of spaces aimed at children and families, illustrating global history. There are also offices, workshops and conference facilities and car parking on the lowest of the three floors. Besides the original brewery walls on the south and east, the west side is a completely new load-bearing structure – 450mm of brick and Stanton stone. The tented structure is of PTFE fabric, made by the same US firm that supplied it for the Millennium Dome in London. A closure flap attaches this fabric to the glass walls and allows for vertical movement of the fabric by up to 1 metre.

It is disconcerting that the three discrete structures seem to be disconnected in form and ignorant of one another's functions. They are like the iron and clay toes of Nebuchadnezzar's dream: they may cleave but they will not incorporate. Thus the amphitheatre and the tent especially are left forlorn, evidently without any real organising principle to their space, and ultimately with all the charm of a motorway service station.

ADDRESS Holyrood Road
ENGINEERS Ove Arup & Partners
CONTRACT VALUE £15 million
BUS 24, 25
ACCESS open

Michael Hopkins & Partners 1998

Michael Hopkins & Partners 1998

Barclay House (The Scotsman Building)

A new headquarters to house the editorial, administrative and management functions of Scotsman Publications Ltd, this is a three-storey building with an open-ended atrium cutting right through from the urban frontage on Holyrood Road to the shelved terraces stepping down to face the Salisbury Crags.

The Holyrood Road façade has three bays forming a concrete curve on each side of the fully glazed atrium. The concrete frame is clad in Rockingstone and Yorkstone. The wrought-iron representation of the thistle and the glass 'Scotsman' lettering above the front door are by blacksmith Paul Johnson. The roofscape, with its tern-coated steel over the entranceway, and the long curved glass of the atrium echo the clean linearity of the lead roof on the Royal High School on Calton Hill.

The interior office space runs down either side of the building; stairways and bridges connect across the atrium. The long-span concrete troughs with exposed soffits aim for energy efficiency through thermal inertia. Extra uplighting has been designed by Jonathan Speirs. Ventilation comes from below with air carried to vents along an underfloor void.

The poplar- and oak-lined boardroom was designed in partnership with Ben Dawson and is spoiled by some tacky art-deco finishing (at the behest of the Barclay brothers, owners of *The Scotsman*).

ADDRESS 108 Holyrood Road
CLIENT Scotsman Properties Ltd
ENGINEER Blyth & Blyth
SIZE 10,700 square metres (115,200 square feet)
BUS 24, 25
ACCESS view from exterior

Comprehensive Design Group Ltd 1999

Barclay House (The Scotsman Building)

Old Town: Holyrood South

Comprehensive Design Group Ltd 1999

St John's Hill Housing

This terrace of housing provides 67 flats for four housing associations, 40 student flats, the Cowgate Day Centre and a five-storey underground car park set into the hill (and only visible here by the two entrance/exit rotundas). As with the Holyrood North site (see page 2.2) there is an emphasis here on the vertical and on the north–south axis. The north–south ridges are higher and slated, while the lower east–west roofs are pantiled.

The use of coloured render here is not as successful as in some parts of the Holyrood site. The designers have not been brave enough to risk putting bold colours together, always separating them – a block of red, a block of cream, a block of blue, and so on – such that it seems somehow too formalised.

ADDRESS St John's Hill/Pleasance/Holyrood
CLIENT Morrison Developments Ltd
ACCESS view from exterior

Gray Marshall & Associates 1998

Gray Marshall & Associates 1998

Old Town South

Tailors' Hall (now the Three Sisters) and Kincaid's Court

On looking down from the George IV Bridge into the Cowgate it's easy to imagine how life in this city brought R L Stevenson to his dualistic nightmare of Jekyll and Hyde. The improved nineteenth-century town with its wide boulevards and neo-classical frontages straddles the dirty dark dens of the Old Town alleyways, yet there's no doubting which is the poets' favourite.

The eighteenth-century city poet Claudero said of the improvements, 'And by degrees each ancient place/will perish by this modern race'. Robert Fergusson in the same century claimed, 'Auld Reekie! Thou'rt the canty hole!', and the Nobel-prize-winning Italian Eugenio Montale, in his poem to Edinburgh in the 1940s wrote, 'The great bridge did not lead to you./I would have reached you even by sailing/through the sewers'. Perhaps it was just such a poetic impulse that led the architects and developers to choose an old courtyard building in the dark canyon of the Cowgate as the site for the bacchanalian and romantic rituals associated with the institution of a super-pub.

Tailors' Hall, a seventeenth-century building, was part of a former brewery which was continually enlarged, altered and re-equipped right up until its closure in the 1970s. The original complex included a pended tenement fronting the Cowgate and enclosing the courtyard and existing building to the north. This tenement was demolished in 1940 leaving the courtyard open to the street.

None of the original upper floors of the Hall, which have been converted to offices and rooms, survive and the two storeys with iron framed vaults to the rear have been converted to bar/restaurants with themed interiors. The building on the east side of the courtyard has been converted to a hotel.

Davis Duncan Harrold Architects 1999

Tailors' Hall (now the Three Sisters) and Kincaid's Court

Old Town South

Davis Duncan Harrold Architects 1999

Tailors' Hall (now the Three Sisters) and Kincaid's Court

The original tenements to the east were demolished and replaced by a new building providing 40 student flats on six floors. Kincaid's Court is a series of vernacular-style tenements individuated by a stepped frontage to the Cowgate, and featuring gablets, blue/black panelled galleries, clerestorey windows, overhanging eaves, and a stylised corner chimney piece.

Retail units at the corner and under the stone and steel-post arcading have proved difficult to let: their unwelcoming proximity to the road is only put into relief by the busy Three Sisters courtyard. The contrast on the streetscape between the smooth modern rendered frontages and the heavy rubble effect of the El Cid-style castellated rear of the Chambers Street Law Courts is also very marked.

A pend leads from Guthrie Street into car parking at the rear of the U-shaped plan.

ADDRESS Cowgate
CLIENTS Burrell Company (Tailors') and Edinburgh University (Kincaid's)
ACCESS bar open to monied young; public hotel open for bookings

Davis Duncan Harrold Architects 1999

Tailors' Hall (now the Three Sisters) and Kincaid's Court

Davis Duncan Harrold Architects 1999

The Dance Base

Malcolm Fraser is not only the designer of the Poetry Library and this Dance Base but also a poet and dancer himself. These factual details will be clear to anyone who studies the plans for the new regional dance centre for Edinburgh based at the Grassmarket.

From the entrance through the pend in an existing building, the four studios lead us on an architectural promenade catering for the full experiential range of dance. The principal studio sits within fragments of old tenement walls and, as it is designed under the influence of traditional Western dance whose impulse is always upwards, it has a fully glazed roof with inspirational views of the castle. The final studio is influenced by African dance and its relationship to the earth; it has therefore been dug right into the basalt of the Castle Rock, has an oversailing roof and looks back down to the Grassmarket. Another studio is on the top floor of the Grassmarket building, and the other at the top of the hill is pavilion roofed with a glass cuboid lantern and a performance garden.

Fraser's scheme is to open a new close as a fire escape going up the hill from the Grassmarket to Johnston Terrace. Thus he not only opens the possibility of reuse for this fallow part of the old city but at the same time creates a new close continuing the Vennel from the other side of the Grassmarket, and also reinstates a part of the old Flodden Wall. The old drying greens to the west of this close are also to be opened as a park.

ADDRESS Grassmarket
CONTRACT VALUE £4.25 million
BUS 2, 35

Malcolm Fraser Architects 2001

Malcolm Fraser Architects 2001

Point Hotel

Both T P Marwick's gushet building of 1914 (the 'point' in question) and his son T W Marwick's 1937 addition (with the first sheer glazed curtain wall in Edinburgh) had lain empty since St Cuthbert's Co-op department store closed in 1987. This closure contributed much to the rundown state of the area during those years, but in 1994 Andrew Doolan acquired the buildings and, in line with the city council's aim to regenerate the corridor from Haymarket to the Grassmarket, decided to develop them into reasonably priced hotel accommodation.

The 130 en-suite bedrooms with very stylish chiaroscuro minimalist decor are on the street façade and wrapped around the curve on the 'point'; all have castle views . Each floor has a spacious bare-walled lobby coded in a bright colour with low-lighting from discrete fluorescent tubes by artist Dan Flavin. The glass curtain wall has been reinstated with the original bronze frame, with a white screen wall behind to provide privacy.

The ground-floor restaurant with its sheer white drapes, dark wood and subdued lighting creates an almost *film-noir* ambience. The chandeliers are modelled on those in the Obecní Dům in Prague. The bar is classic Parisian with a curved bar and hard surfaces, all reflecting light and noise. The reception between the bar and restaurant leads along a yellow wall to the foyer where the guests entering have their first meditatively minimalist experience as they wait for the lift. A new penthouse suite on top of the St Cuthbert's building was completed in September 2000.

ADDRESS Bread Street
CLIENT Dance Base
BUS 35
ACCESS bar and restaurant open to public; hotel open for bookings

Andrew Doolan Architects 1995–99

Andrew Doolan Architects 1995–99

The Exchange

The Exchange

Is Terry Farrell the long-lost mad bastard great-great-grandson of 'Greek' Thomson? This must be the question on all Glaswegians' lips as they speed eastwards along the Western Approach Road following the great Scottish cultural brain drain of the late 1990s and early new millennium.

In 1989 London architect Terry Farrell won the competition to design the masterplan for the sprawling 9-acre wasteland between the Western Approach Road and Morrison Street, the former Caledonian Railway Station and Goods Yard. Farrell's plan was required to create a new financial centre with office space catering for the needs of large corporations; a much-needed conference centre, designed by himself; car parking; a leisure centre for the Sheraton; and a public square, all around the two existing buildings on Festival Square – the Sheraton and Capital House.

His design not only seeks to join the Old and New Towns but also to link public spaces by the provision of north–south and east–west cycle and pedestrian routes through the site.

While the influence of nineteenth-century Glaswegian architect Alexander 'Greek' Thomson – his post-and-lintel emphasis on the horizontal and his neo-classical incorporation of elements of every style from Greek to Egyptian – on the actual design of the buildings is clear enough, it must be said that the worst excesses are not perpetrated by Farrell but the Exchange Plaza curving round the bend of the Western Approach Road. As the *Architectural Review* put it, 'a rash of passé po-mo erupted from the west end, the outbreak apparently being started by Terry Farrell's Conference Centre, which is a jewel of decorum compared to some of the recent loutish offerings'.

ADDRESS Lothian Road

Terry Farrell and Partners (masterplanner) 1989

Terry Farrell and Partners (masterplanner) 1989

Edinburgh International Conference Centre and Conference House

The basic external form of the building is of a 25-metre-tall circular drum with four smaller corner blocks. Their scale anchors the massive drum in the tenement cityscape – especially that on the south side of Morrison Street. The buff-coloured concrete façade is punctured with horizontal bands of regular rhythmic openings and, together with the oversailing perforated metal cornice, it is a circular form not only recognisable in the context of urban Edinburgh but also in an historical context. With its rhythm of openings round the façade, the Coliseum in Rome is one model that comes immediately to mind. Another, for the same reason and also because of its similar use of smaller-scale pavilions to anchor it in the cityscape, is Ledoux's Barrière de la Villette in Paris.

The entrance to the building from Morrison Street is a *tour de force*, with a steel-framed fabric portico sweeping down in front of a two-and-a-half storey glass curtain wall enclosing the stairway and escalators. The wave-shaped steel beams of the portico cantilever out from the façade, secured from windlift by rod ties at their ends, and hold the fabric in an upside-down tented form. Pipes from the inverted peaks of these tents drain the rainwater down into the steel columns.

The structure of the building, like a bicycle wheel, consists of a central drum framed in steelwork with radial beams supported at the centre and around the perimeter by circular steel columns.

The principal spaces are stacked vertically, with a drop of 8 metres from the Morrison Street entry to the basement floor with an exhibition/banqueting hall and vehicle entrance under the raised deck of Conference Square from the Western Approach Road. Other floors contain breakout rooms, offices, committee rooms and foyers, with the main auditorium on the top floor. Edinburgh District Council research had shown that the

Terry Farrell and Partners 1995

Terry Farrell and Partners 1995

optimum conference market for the city lay in the 800–1 200-person high-tech and medical sectors. Thus the brief for this building called for a 1 200-seater auditorium capable of quick and easy subdivision. Farrell solved this problem masterfully by having two smaller drums at the rear of the auditorium, each seating 300, which can rotate on a circular rail, turning their back wall to the principal space of 600. Thus a great flexibility in terms of size of audience and number of simultaneous talks/conferences is made possible. The cherry-wood panelling which is found throughout the building also lines the walls of the auditoria in a particular rhythmic design reminiscent of the façade and enhancing the harmony of the piece.

Conference House is a 30,500-square-foot office block designed alongside the EICC to a more strictly tenemental scale, in blond and red sandstone and echoing the curved block on the corner of Gardner's Crescent.

ADDRESS Morrison Street
CLIENT Edinburgh International Conference Centre
ENGINEER Ove Arup & Partners
CONTRACT VALUE £33.4 million
BUS 2, 35
ACCESS view from exterior; conference facilities available for booking

Terry Farrell and Partners 1995

Edinburgh International Conference Centre and Conference House

The Exchange

Terry Farrell and Partners 1995

Edinburgh One

A steel-framed superstructure with composite concrete upper floors and concrete basement retaining walls. This building has four streetside floors clad in Clashach sandstone, respecting tenement height, and two stepped-back fully glazed floors above. The tower echoes other obvious motifs in the street; the curve on the façade answers back to Conference House.

While the street side of this building contains open-plan offices, to the north is a fully automated car park capable of housing 610 cars. This is the first of its type in the UK, and is designed for security, the automation ensuring that no one should have to take a solitary walk round a dark multi-storey car park at night to retrieve their vehicle.

ADDRESS Morrison Street
CLIENTS Mercury Asset Management Property Division, Parlison Properties and SkyParks
CONTRACT VALUE £15 million
SIZE 5000 square metres (54,000 square feet)
BUS 2, 35
ACCESS view from exterior

Hurd Rolland Partnership 2000

Hurd Rolland Partnership 2000

Sheraton Hotel Health Club

Sited behind the Sheraton Hotel and forming the eastern edge of Conference Square, this building is constructed over the two storeys of car parking under the square. Accommodation includes two rooftop swimming pools, hydrotherapy and beauty suites, gymnasia and exercise rooms, bars, restaurants and retail space. Farrell and Partners completed the shell of the building by 2000, and the interior fit out by Syntex was to be completed by summer 2001.

A concrete-and-glass-walled box, it comes as a relief from the heaviness of all the surrounding neo-classical façades and enlivens Conference Square in a way that is entirely unexpected. It charges into a tight and very uncompromising site, its northern concrete and louvred wall coming within 12 metres of the Clydesdale Plaza façade to form the apex of the roughly triangular public space.

This proximity of stone façades would be merely unwelcoming, not to say threatening, to pedestrians approaching that opening to the square were it not for the clever way the off-rectilinear geometry of the building has been handled. The ground floor is completely glass walled with accommodation for shops, bars, etc., and the concrete box overhangs this so that pedestrians have visual access through the building to the irregularly shaped and sloped Conference Square opening out in front of them.

A part of the main Sheraton Hotel complex which lies to its east, the buildings communicate via a glassed bridge on the top floor and steps from the spa entrance hall lead down to the hotel's main road entrance. The health club does, however, maintain its own identity, and the form and a palette of materials combine to give it a light, transparent, aquatic style. Both east and west façades are completely glazed with blue and green ceramic fritting providing shade, colour and play of light. The fish-shaped curve of the feature containing the outdoor pool cantilevers out

Terry Farrell and Partners 2001

Terry Farrell and Partners 2001

from the upper storey clad in a microrib of mica flip finish which looks brown/grey in shade but has a scaly blue green aquatic shimmer in the sun.

This building can be placed as part of Farrell's modernist experimentation which took in such other glass-walled projects as his retail and clinic buildings for Korea. Yet there's more to it than that. Once inside we find that the heavy concrete pillars and the stepped section of the floors not only contribute to the effect of the play of light, but clearly are involved in some special promenade. We go round concrete pillars, up ramps and steps, across gymnasia, passing sequestered therapy rooms, through the cat flap to the outdoor heated pool. We find ourselves in some neo-Roman baths here with all the classical order of their promenade: frigidarium, tepidarium, caldarium, palestrae, etc. The similarity in plan between the Baths of Caracalla in Rome, with their caldarium rotunda protruding on the long side and opening up the centrally planned rectangle, and this Health Club with its hot outdoor pool cantilevered out from the top floor, is striking.

But perhaps we ought not to be surprised to find this thoroughly researched basis to one of Farrell's ostensibly stylised buildings. As Duncan Whatmore (in charge of Farrell's Edinburgh office) says of the evolution of their architecture: 'we think of it as different analytical processes rather than different styles'. That seems a mature approach, but as masterplanners is it too much to ask of other design architects?

ADDRESS Conference Square
CLIENT Cheval Property Management.
CONTRACT VALUE £3.2 million
SIZE 4900 square metres (52,700 square feet)
BUS 2, 35

Terry Farrell and Partners 2001

The Exchange

Exchange Plaza and Crescent

The Exchange Plaza (now renamed Clydesdale Plaza by the occupier) is the building on Lothian Road and the Western Approach Road that completes Festival Square and forms the southern half of the gateway to the city (opposite Standard Life House; see page 5.18) required by Terry Farrell's masterplan. A quarter rotunda entrance way, glazed on the upper floors, is sandwiched between two sandstone-clad rectilinear towers with turrets on top.

Exchange Crescent, clad in the same stone with the same detailing, curves from the Plaza building round the edge of the Western Approach Road, enclosing Conference Square on its inner side. The crescent is centred on a pair of towers which signal the pedestrian entranceway by the steel bridge from Rutland Square through the building to Conference Square. Round the Conference Square side a glass-roofed portico is held up by pillars of that Terry Farrell-style mixture of neo-classical stonework and high-tech metalwork.

These postmodern classical-fronted office buildings, though seemingly much influenced by Alexander Thomson in their trabeated form, have none of what he called 'the mysterious power of the horizontal element', and have been much criticised. In *The History of Scottish Architecture* by Glendinning *et al* we read that they are 'vastly inflated' and they featured in the Outrage page of the *Architectural Review* which said: 'No-one doubts the necessity for big buildings in one of Europe's most successful financial capitals, but do they all have to be so brash, over-scaled and assertive?'

While most of the criticism does focus on the sheer size and bulk of these buildings, it must be said in their defence that there are reasons for this scale – the call for gateway buildings in Farrell's masterplan, the respect for eaves height of neighbouring buildings and so on – most of

Cochrane McGregor 1998 and 2000

Cochrane McGregor 1998 and 2000

5.16

which are set out below in a discussion of the other 'gateway' building, Standard Life House. But the real disappointment about these buildings must be the style in which that scale was achieved. Their attempt to find an Edinburgh 'classical elegance' through postmodern detailing of sandstone façades has been for a long time, as the *Architectural Review* says, 'passé' and the last sentence should be left to them: 'Surely a city that was once the wonder of the civilised world deserves better than such vulgar provincial banalities'.

The Exchange

ADDRESS Lothian Road/Western Approach Road
ENGINEERS phases 1 and 2, Cundall Johnston & Partners; phase 3, Woolgar Hunter
CONTRACT VALUE £40 million
SIZE 28,800 square metres (310,000 square feet)
ACCESS view from exterior; access through pend from Conference Square to steel bridge

Cochrane McGregor 1998 and 2000

Cochrane McGregor 1998 and 2000

Standard Life House

The designers of this building at the junction of a busy city thoroughfare and a major entryway to the city centre had to meet a complex set of requirements from the various interested parties. Standard Life, the client, is Europe's biggest mutual life assurance firm, whose business has grown 800 per cent since 1975, and they wanted a new headquarters building that would be 'forward looking, from a secure and traditional base'. City planning regulations determined certain restrictions on height and on sightlines, while the Terry Farrell masterplan for the area (see page 5.2) required that there be a major building sited here with tower elements forming a gateway to the city together with the building on the south side of this junction. In addition to these conditions, the masterplan required cycle and pedestrian access through to Rutland Square, and there was also the problem presented by a major railway tunnel that passed under the site.

The resultant design is of one building with two wings, east and west, which are joined by a full six-storey bridge over a pedestrian access from the corner of the junction through to Rutland Square. The rotunda of entrance steps and gates to the pedestrian passageway were designed by sculptor John Maine.

The two wings – the parallelogram-shaped plan of the eastern which faces on to Lothian Road, and the triangular plan around a central atrium of the western which faces on to the Western Approach Road – form 40,000 square metres of office space on six floors and two penthouse floors. The floor plate has a depth of 16.8 metres. On the exterior the first three floors are clad in natural stone with regular window openings; the three intermediate floors have freestanding stone-clad columns fronting a glass curtain wall, and above the cornice level is a copper-clad storey whose roof finish matches that of the Usher Hall. The gateway

Michael Laird Partnership 1996

Michael Laird Partnership 1996

Standard Life House

elements on the corner are the towers surmounted by octagonal rooms and copper-clad domes which, with their finials, look almost like something atop a Turkish mosque. The pedestrian access through the site is completed by a steel bridge designed by Terry Farrell which runs from Rutland Square on the west side of this building over the Western Approach Road to Exchange Crescent.

One ever-present concern about this building is the question of scale. Quite a few splashes of tar land here from the *Architectural Review*'s broad brush criticising the scale and assertiveness of the buildings in The Exchange (see page 5.14).

Perhaps for once we can learn something about buildings and the design impulse behind them by looking for an allegorical level, conscious or not, in the art works that are commissioned for them. The 'first tangible action by the City Council, following publication of the Proposals' (Charles McKean) which gave us the order and clarity of the New Town was to build the City Chambers in the High Street, a u-plan hotel by the Adams in 1751. In the courtyard of the City Chambers is a statue by Steele of Alexander, the great Greek leader, with Bucephalus, his horse, whom legend has it, was not only controlled by, but was also a friend of Alexander. Meanwhile on the raised deck between Standard Life House and the Baillie Gifford building to the west, just before Farrell's bridge, is another equestrian statue by Eoghan Bridge. In this work the beast is completely out of control, and clearly far too big and powerful for the rider, who is a mere boy. Does that contrast say something for this whole Exchange development in terms of scale, vision, ability and maturity?

The architects nonetheless have ready answers for these questions. They can point to the step-back on levels four and six on the rear of this building, designed so that it does not affect the sightlines or required

Michael Laird Partnership 1996

Michael Laird Partnership 1996

daylight angle to Rutland Square. They were, of course, required by the masterplanner to build a major gateway building to the city, and they have done so in a way which also respects the ridge and cornice levels of its neighbour, the Caledonian Hotel. But then perhaps that is no great achievement. Whoever said that the Caledonian Hotel was an Edinburgh-sized or Edinburgh-coloured building anyway?

ADDRESS Lothian Road
CLIENT Standard Life Assurance Company
ENGINEER Blyth & Blyth
CONTRACT VALUE £62.5 million
SIZE 40,000 square metres (430,500 square feet)
ACCESS view from exterior, access through passageway to Rutland Square

Michael Laird Partnership 1996

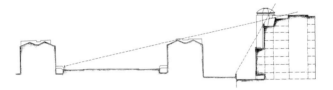

Standard Life House

The Exchange

Michael Laird Partnership 1996

Scottish Widows

It seems right to have a monument to Scottish Widows built here at Port Hamilton, for this is the site where Burke and Hare, murderers of 16 Edinburgh people in 1827, worked on the canals. Unfortunately, the Scottish Widows in question is merely an international company providing financial services, and the building, though of great size and some geometrical complexity, is hardly monumental. So much for romance.

The architects describe this collection of buildings as being in the form of a 'crescent, courtyard and screen'. The curved glazed wall of the crescent soars at least two floors above the surrounding buildings and is fronted by an atrium, held between the crescent and two wings which form tangents to the crescent and meet at a right angle on the street front. A double basement of in-situ reinforced concrete houses car parks. The architects point out that the façades in honey-coloured precast concrete, with Clashach stone cladding and bronze-coloured silicon-glazed windows and arcades on 'balanced beams', reflect the interior concern for exposed thermal mass and energy efficiency.

This building seems to turn away from the street and adds nothing to the city council's attempt to reinstate Morrison Street as a major entry route to the city. Perhaps that is just as well for its façades with their pillars, arcaded ground-floor windows, clerestorey gallery, overhanging barrel roofs, oriel windows, rotundas, bronze panelling and sandstone cladding might be too chaotic to line a major thoroughfare.

The point is that this huge crescent-shaped building, while claimed to be 'subject to the strong influence of the city's unique urban fabric', does not, like Farrell's or Benson and Forsyth's rotundas, take part in the city, but hides away (probably for shame at its size). It is only really viewed fully from up on the Castle Esplanade where it is seen soaring above everything, relating to nothing, like some ridiculous Kilroy.

Building Design Partnership 1997

Building Design Partnership 1997

How did such a building gain planning permission? Port Hamilton is just outside the existing city-centre conservation area but nonetheless the council was very reluctant to give it the go-ahead. The story goes that Michael Ross, head of Scottish Widows – whose headquarters was formerly on Dalkeith Road – went through to Glasgow to look at the vacant former Britoil Offices on St Vincent Street. 'I made sure I was seen, and that people whispered in the ears of the city fathers', he said (*Evening News*, October 1999).

The rest is not only history, but history repeating itself. For if the snaffling of the prime site (intended for a church) in St Andrews Square for Sir Laurence Dundas' villa in the 1770s represented 'the triumph of land ownership over good planning' (Charles McKean), then the building of this Scottish Widows headquarters is simply the contempt of corporate power for local democracy.

At least Dundas left us with a fine (if wrongly sited) building as penance for his corrupt ways.

ADDRESS Port Hamilton
CLIENT Edinburgh Construction Services
ENGINEERS W A Fairhurst & Partners
CONTRACT £66 million
SIZE 32,600 square metres (351,000 square feet)
BUS 2, 35
ACCESS view from exterior

Building Design Partnership 1997

Building Design Partnership 1997

Tollcross

Tollcross

Percy Johnson-Marshall and Partners produced a masterplan for the derelict east side of Tollcross, including the former site of Goldbergs department store, in 1995. The plan incorporated student accommodation, private and public housing, and a commercial office development, with pedestrian routes through the sites and civic spaces. Student accommodation for Napier University, private housing for Tulloch Homes and a car-free housing-association development have already been created, and the Princes Exchange (see page 6.4) is the final phase.

Percy Johnson-Marshall and Partners (masterplanners) 1995

Percy Johnson-Marshall and Partners (masterplanners) 1995

Princes Exchange

Princes Exchange is a five- and six-storey steel-framed office development along the edges of High Riggs, Earl Grey Street and Lauriston Place with a corner drum tower as a main focus to the Lauriston Street/Lothian Road junction. A convex façade at the Tollcross junction forms the entrance to the remainder of the building, and fronts on to a new south-facing civic space. The floorplates are 15 metres deep and have floor-to-ceiling glazing with flat silver cladding panels and *brises-soleils* between the exposed steel structure. The aluminium standing-seam roof encloses penthouse executive areas.

The office accommodation, which stands on a site owned jointly by the Bank of Scotland and the Royal Bank of Scotland, was 50 per cent prelet to the Bank of Scotland in 1998.

ADDRESS Tollcross
CLIENT Teesland
CONTRACT VALUE £27 million
SIZE 18,600 square metres (200,000 square feet)
BUS 11, 15, 16, 17, 23, 27, 45
ACCESS view from exterior

Percy Johnson-Marshall and Partners 2000

Percy Johnson-Marshall and Partners 2000

High Riggs

This development of 63 flats on a triangular site is rendered in an eye-catching yellow, with a six-storey-high flat-fronted gushet tower facing Tollcross. These flats were the first completed car-free scheme in Edinburgh, with parking spaces provided only for essential services. A pedestrian route passes through a pend from Lauriston Place to the pedestrianised High Riggs, where there are private walled gardens.

Disappointing is the Lauriston Street end of this development where the gap left between it and the Jesuit church of the Sacred Heart doesn't balance the Roman baroque joint on the other side with its curving cornice, windows and doorways in a study of solid and void.

ADDRESS Lauriston Place
CLIENT Dunedin Housing Association
BUS 23, 27
ACCESS various pedestrian routes through site; café open to public on ground-floor gushet

Campbell & Arnott Architects 1999

Campbell & Arnott Architects 1999

Southside

Museum of Scotland

The modern has been said to be a state of mind, to be a change in the conception of the relation of the human to his or her object world. Under this definition, with modern architecture as a direct and anti-classical relating of spaces and solids to the subject, the severest critic might say that there are only two completed modern buildings by Scottish architects in Scotland.

If we admit one of them to be the new Museum of Scotland then the other would have to be St Peter's Seminary, Cardross, designed by Isi Metzstein of Gillespie Kidd & Coia (GKC) in the late 1950s and early 1960s. Both buildings have an oblique curtain or retaining wall with a cylinder tower form on one corner, and the bulk of the building situated on the perpendicular behind that wall with floors organised around a central longitudinal atrium. But the similarities in the design and plans of these buildings should come as no surprise: on at least two occasions (opening an exhibition on GKC at the Architectural Association in London, and in his inaugural professorial address at the University of Strathclyde) Gordon Benson has pointed to the influence of GKC, as well as Mackintosh and Le Corbusier, on his work.

The original competition was merely for an extension which would be fully integrated with Fowke's original Royal Museum. In fact, this £60 million completed building has its own distinct function and entrance while still being linked to its Chambers Street neighbour.

The difficulty on this tight square site has been to place a large building that could subtly negotiate its way between the horizontality of Fowke's elongated Italian palazzo on Chambers Street and the vertical orientation of the Edinburgh tenements around Greyfriars. This has been done by wrapping a lower outer building, hung with a rainscreen of Clashach sandstone, around the higher main galleries inside. This wall, together

Benson and Forsyth 1998

Southside

Benson and Forsyth 1998

with the corner cylindrical entrance tower (and the somewhat armorial Ivanhoe-helmet-style incisions in its stone) deliberately invoke the metaphor of the Scottish castle. The tower itself not only gathers all five roads into the entrance of the museum, and mirrors the half-moon battery of the castle, but also helps obscure the abrupt step down of the wall from Chambers Street to George IV Bridge.

Visitors penetrate through the circular entry hall of the tower into the triangular, sloped-floor reception area, and on into the inner core beyond that outer ring. They find themselves immediately confronted with a variety of different forms of space connected to or separated from each other in a seemingly infinite number of ways: bridges, windows, ramps, viewing platforms, atriums, stairways, balconies, etc. Visitors are invited by these 'layering transparencies' to find their own way through the building, relating spaces to one another, and hence making their own links between the different parts of the collection. Thus the architects let us make our own connections between the different narratives and disciplines in history, demonstrating that the Scottish generalist principle – the democratic intellect – not only can, but must be the modern way.

Once out on the roof in the white concrete boat-shaped garden above the Clashach stone wall there is a 360-degree view. The visitor can put together all those glimpses of Edinburgh caught through windows from the interior by orientating the museum precisely in the cityscape.

Despite fulsome praise this building has had its problems. It had a history of difficulties in terms of finding funding and support before a stone was even laid. The building has also had its critics. Prince Charles let it be known that he opposed the execution of this design, and when he was asked what he thought of the finished building said simply that he didn't comment on buildings on Wednesdays. It failed to be shortlisted

Benson and Forsyth 1998

Southside

Benson and Forsyth 1998

for an RIBA award with one panel judge saying it was 'overwrought and excessive' and another claiming that he would 'defy anyone who goes there and looks at it without nationalist baggage to say that it is a world-class building'.

While this latter opinion is only an extrapolation of Charles' midweek subjectivism, there are, apart from minor problems like shoddy interior detailing, also some inconsistencies in the design. Do you not sometimes get the feeling (as from the interior balconies overlooking Hawthornden Court) that this building is sometimes too self-regarding, that it is made to show off itself rather than the collection? There is also an oppressive amount of ironic architectural quotation such as the Corbusian Ronchamp windows with flimsy wooden-panel interior sloping sills, instead of thick walls. As one critic in the *The Architects' Journal* wrote, 'the originals seem to overshadow their appropriators'. These effects seem to be made to impress the cognoscenti. Their self-referentiality and irony only detract from that above-mentioned 'democratic' ideal.

ADDRESS Chambers Street/George IV Bridge
CLIENT The Board of Trustees of the National Museums of Scotland
ENGINEER Anthony Hunt Associates
CONTRACT VALUE £60 million
BUS 23, 27, 28, 40, 41, 42
ACCESS open

Benson and Forsyth 1998

Southside

Benson and Forsyth 1998

Student Centre

An extension to the original student centre of 1966–73 by the same architects, a channelled sandstone screen wall with drum and a stairway wrapped around it give an air of monumental mystery. Inside though is a new multipurpose hall, refreshment lounges and changing facilities. The architects have respected the wishes of Professor Johnson Marshall, designer of Bristo Square, that from the steps of McEwan Hall you should be able to see the dome on the Old Quad.

ADDRESS Bristo Square
CLIENT University of Edinburgh
BUS 40, 41, 42
ACCESS open to students

Morris & Steadman 1997

Morris & Steadman 1997

Mosque and Islamic Centre

A hybrid of Scots and Islamic architecture, the architect always had an eye on Scots forms, and a feel for the materials – sandstone, copper, slate – while adapting them freely with the Muslim anti-iconographic penchant for extravagant geometry. Each of the four corners has an octagonal Holyrood-style tower echoing those of Sydney Mitchell & Wilson's students union building on the other side of Bristo Square (in Teviot Place). Three of the towers are topped with hexagonal candle-snuffer roofs – making the building at least 75 per cent Scots, if quantification is necessary in this mathematical environment – and the other sprouts a heavy copper-cupola'd minaret. Overall Al-Bayati demonstrates some understanding of the traditional massing of Scottish architecture in this piece. There are also some geometrical versions of Scots corbelling to the square turrets to the rear and in the interior. The building houses a large prayer room, a multipurpose hall, a smaller prayer room for women, a library and offices. It has traditionally plain interiors.

The eighteenth-century Chapel House behind has been totally eclipsed by the new building and it now forms part of the mosque with kitchens and spaces for classrooms, and for washing the dead.

ADDRESS Buccleuch Street
BUS 40, 41, 42
BUS open
ACCESS open

Basil Al-Bayati 1998

Basil Al-Bayati 1998

Buccleuch Street Housing

This tenement block contains 18 flats, and through the pend a further six flats in mews-type buildings around car-parking space. Entrance to all tenement flats is by a single curved stairtower, also through the pend, and open-access balconies. The terracotta rendering above the cast-stone base is a lively element in the street, and a certain vertical emphasis – in an arrangement of fenestration, cobalt blue ceramic tile inserts, and dormer upstands – makes it up to its taller northern neighbour.

Southside

ADDRESS 59–69 Buccleuch Street
CLIENT Edinvar Housing Association
CONTRACT VALUE £750,000
BUS 40, 41, 42
ACCESS view from exterior

Percy Thomas Partnership 1992

Percy Thomas Partnership 1992

Festival Theatre

There has been talk – indeed debate and dispute – over the building of an opera house in Edinburgh since the festival started in 1947. Law & Dunbar-Naismith were first asked by the council in 1975 to take a look at the possibility of converting the old Empire theatre into an opera house capable of staging major international productions. The theatre, however, remained in use as a bingo hall until 1988. (James Dunbar-Naismith is said to have become a member of Mecca in order to gain regular access.)

This is the oldest surviving theatrical site in Edinburgh: eight previous structures date back as far as the eighteenth century. The oldest part of the present building was the south wall of Frank Matcham's 1892 building whose stage burnt down in 1911, killing the famous illusionist Lafayette, his lion, and eight others in his entourage. Lafayette was paranoid about 'spies' stealing his tricks, and had made sure all the stage doors were locked during performance. Thus his fate too was sealed for he had no possible escape from the fire.

Law & Dunbar-Naismith's intervention involves both extremities of the theatre with the 1928 Millburn brothers' auditorium more or less left untouched apart from some colour changes and new seating arrangements. A new unraked stage twice the size of the original has been built. It is now the biggest in the country and has an adjustable orchestra pit trebled in size (120 musicians). A scene dock beyond the stage has also been created which can be acoustically isolated so that work can be carried on during performances. There has been criticism of the resulting exterior bulk of the backstage and fly tower but the architects hope that new development will obscure this.

The other principal work was carried out on the front of house and foyer. The circulation spaces have been altered and simplified and a three-

Law & Dunbar-Naismith 1994

Southside

Law & Dunbar-Naismith 1994

floor, full-height curving glass façade has been added. The glass assembly system is hung from a concrete ring beam at roof level with slender bow trusses. This wall not only throws an open welcome out to the passer-by but has a verticality that draws the eyes up from the grey canyon of the street. It turns, as one critic put it, 'the meanness of the awkward site to its advantage'.

When the architects state as preface to their work on the front of house that theatre includes experience outside the performance, it is mercifully not poor Lafayette they have in mind but foyer-life. Anyone who has read Balzac knows of theatre-going as a way of life in parts of the Continent.

'Successful foyer design', say Law & Dunbar-Naismith, 'is to create the quickest route from seat to bar'. Is this why it is called the vomitorium? The simple and serious reason for this is that the bar is where the theatre makes most money, so why not make it accessible, bright, open and pleasant? By their own standards the architects have succeeded: from the foyers there are views out to Playfair's Surgeons' Hall and beyond to the Salisbury Crags, and past Adam's University all the way down the bridges to his Register House. The only let-down comes when this panoramic effect occasionally suffers a blind disappointment as posters, lanterns and such trivia are hung across the façade.

ADDRESS Nicolson Street
CLIENT Edinburgh Festival Theatre Trust
CONTRACT VALUE £16.5 million
BUS 3, 5, 7, 8, 14, 21, 31, 33, 80, 81, 82
ACCESS open to public

Law & Dunbar-Naismith 1994

Law & Dunbar-Naismith 1994

New Town

Princes Street Galleries

What is there worth preserving in Princes Street? There are very few buildings of quality and the whole street seems a bit of a hotch-potch. Writer and journalist Moray McLaren once said it was 'one of the most chaotically tasteless streets in the United Kingdom'.

Nonetheless the battle over the development of Princes Street has been going for a long time. In the 1770s fourteen residents of the New Town, including David Hume, took their fight to stop building on the south side of the street to the House of Lords, and after further dispute an Act of Parliament in 1816 prevented any building there for all time to come. Youngson, in his book *The Making of Classical Edinburgh*, comments on this Act: 'Thus was saved, in spite of the town council, the most important asset and true singularity of Edinburgh; the physical separation and the visible conjunction of the Old Town and the New'.

Note there the reference to the town council; once again it is involved in a scheme to develop the street. The Edinburgh Development and Investment (EDI) group is a council-owned property-development company which, together with architects Comprehensive Design, came up with a scheme to introduce half a mile of subterranean shopping malls beneath Princes Street, linking the museums, shops and the station.

'The city needs a decent modern shopping centre at its heart', says Ian Wall of EDI. Comprehensive Design add that the development being underground would nowhere block the 'visible conjunction' of Old and New Towns, with only glazed views from cafés looking down over the gardens. There would also be a £6.3 million competition to regenerate Princes Street itself.

Needless to say, there has been great opposition to the project. At the public enquiry into the plans this opposition was organised by the Cockburn Association (with the support of the Scottish Civic Trust, Architec-

Comprehensive Design Group Ltd 2004

Princes Street Galleries

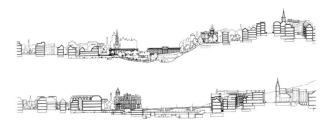

Comprehensive Design Group Ltd 2004

New Town

tural Heritage Society of Scotland, Edinburgh Old Town Association and Central Edinburgh New Town Association). They pointed out that although they are not opposed to the development in principle, they are opposed to the granting of *carte blanche* inasmuch as these are just outline plans and the very authority (Edinburgh City Council) that sits in judgement on planning permission also owns the developer that produced the plans.

Others have raised the question of the aesthetics of building an underground mall of only 3 metres in height, and suggest it would be cramped and unwelcoming. Would it not be better, they say, to revert to something like the R Furneaux Jordan plans for the street, and build a series of glass malls on the north side of the street with excellent views of the Old Town?

A second public enquiry gave the final ruling to the Scottish Executive. They gave a decision against the scheme and appeared to agree with the Cockburn Association that the plans were not detailed enough. The decision did, however, seem to leave open the possibility of a more detailed plan succeeding and EDI is still confident that the development will ultimately go ahead.

Meanwhile, Railtrack Scotland has sought to make changes to that 1816 Act by sponsoring a private member's bill at Westminster. Railtrack want to spend £400 million on a revamp and expansion of Waverley Station, inviting international architects to submit designs to a competition. Its plans entail raising the Waverley roof by up to 2 metres, which would take it above the 42-foot (12.8-metre) maximum height set in the nineteenth-century Act.

One group, CETA (Centre for Ecological Technology and Agriculture), has proposed to Railtrack that the revamped Waverley Station be roofed

Comprehensive Design Group Ltd 2004

with photovoltaic solar panels. It claims that advances in the technology have now made these panels just as cheap to use as materials like concrete. With more than half of the 37,000-square-metre roof surface covered, this would be the largest solar site in the world, creating enough energy to power 140 minibuses for more than 70 kilometres each per day. This could be one answer to the city's pollution problems, but so far Railtrack has shown no interest in the scheme.

ADDRESS Princes Street
CLIENT EDI
CONTRACT VALUE £100 million

Comprehensive Design Group Ltd 2004

Comprehensive Design Group Ltd 2004

One Castle Street

Can a designer make sense of Princes Street? Is it possible for an architect to be enthusiastic or even clear-minded about a project there? One Castle Street, replacing a shop and the Palace Hotel, which burnt down in June 1991, tries a few tricks but is no more successful than its neighbours.

The glass canopy at first-floor level round the building seems to be a half-hearted attempt to pay homage to the projected walkways on other post-war Princes Street buildings (The New Club, 122, 108 and 101–103, etc.) following the prescription of the 1958 plan. Half-hearted also is the echo of the Debenham's bay window in the rotunda above the fifth-floor balcony. The projected bays with flush windows at the corner seek to imitate a tower and give vertical emphasis, while the stone cladding and respect for its neighbour's cornice heights are said to be an advantage.

ADDRESS Castle Street
CLIENT Trafalgar House Developments
ENGINEER Blyth & Blyth
ACCESS shops on ground floor open to public

YRM Architects and Planners 1994

YRM Architects and Planners 1994

10 George Street

Within a 'predictable and barren commercial brief' the architects say that in this project they attempted to 'engage and describe the spirit of the Georgian condition'. That's admirable surely, and for a contemporary steel-framed building with sandstone pillars across the façade, the voids as long pseudo-Georgian windows as opposed to modern glass curtain walling, the oversailing roof as cornice and the handling of the step down from St Andrew's Square to Rhind's Royal Bank (now converted to a bar and restaurant) they certainly seem to be 'engaging' with the New Town environment.

What they are seeking, however, seems to be an anonymous role. 'Edinburgh New Town illustrates a profound demonstration of space-making rather than object-making', they say. Of course, it's George Street as originally intended, a mere telescope to look from the site of Dundas Villa to West Register House and back again.

ADDRESS George Street
CLIENT Life Association of Scotland
CONTRACT VALUE £10 million
ACCESS view from exterior

Reiach & Hall Architects 1995

Reiach & Hall Architects 1995

Pizza Express, Queensferry Road

Through a series of curving motifs – the glass and steel entranceway, and the cherry-wood ribs of the counter – the visitor is led through the building from the narrow entranceway on Queensferry Road and upwards to the light of the upper dining area with its glass doors on to the courtyard in Charlotte Lane. The column in this upper dining area is perhaps the only clumsy note.

ADDRESS Queensferry Road
CLIENT Pizza Express Ltd
ENGINEER Elliot and Co.
SIZE 222 square metres (2400 square feet)
ACCESS open to public

Malcolm Fraser Architects 1997

Pizza Express, Queensferry Road

New Town

Malcolm Fraser Architects 1997

Dublin Street Lane Housing

This housing, like an East Neuk village cross dropped into the backlands of New Town tenements, is an attempt by Richard Murphy to exploit what he calls the 'archaeological significance' of the site.

When the New Town was first mooted the old Broughton village stood here. The plan was to destroy the village and run a new road through, but that never happened and the buildings on site found themselves surrounded, an aberration in the formal grid of New Town tenements.

Murphy won a 1995 competition to design housing for this site providing six two-storey houses and 22 flats, and these more or less preserve the footprint of their predecessors; their materials and forms give a reinterpretation of the medieval. The façades are a mix of rendered masonry walls with small windows and western red cedar boarding around large sliding windows forming balconies with external balustrades. There is a galvanised-steel stairway to the front of each one.

Invoking the old in this way, everything is also very new, with a deliberately tantalising off-symmetry to the play of forms; the different patterns of cutaways and the layering of materials – steel, wood, masonry, slate and glass. Given thus an immediate visual interaction the user feels invited to touch these materials, see where and how they meet, and ultimately how he or she fits into this scheme.

ADDRESS Dublin Street Lane North
CLIENTS Edinburgh Development Investments Ltd and The Burrell Company Ltd
ENGINEER Laird Menzies Partnership
CONTRACT VALUE £1.4 million
ACCESS view from exterior

Richard Murphy Architects 1998

Dublin Street Lane Housing

New Town

Richard Murphy Architects 1998

17 Royal Terrace Mews

Originally a stable with a small cabin above for a stable boy, Richard Murphy has now converted this into a mews house. To obtain planning permission a garage had to be incorporated, so most of the accommodation – the living and sleeping spaces – is on the first floor. Like a conjurer's closet, the ingenious use of sliding panels, cutaways and transparencies, *trompe l'oeil* mirrors, fake correspondences and continuities, creates a dynamic, the purpose of which is to make the flat one continuous, continually evolving space culminating in the bedroom under a trademark rooflight.

ADDRESS 17 Royal Terrace Mews
CLIENTS Jens and Carol Hogel
ENGINEER David Narro Associates
CONTRACT VALUE £96,000
BUS 25
ACCESS view from exterior

Richard Murphy Architects 1995

Richard Murphy Architects 1995

Calton Square, Greenside

This site was intended for a traffic interchange on the inner ring road, and the existing tenements were demolished in 1973. Since the inner ring-road plans were abandoned, several other plans were brought forward for this site. BBC Scotland at one time intended to build its headquarters here with terrace views of Calton Hill, and then there were plans for a development including a hotel, office and shops, which were actually awarded planning permission, and the existing grid and concrete basement car park were built.

Allan Murray Architects won first place in an international competition for this site in 1998 with a design for a leisure complex, an office headquarters building, roof gardens and a new civic square linking with Calton Hill.

ADDRESS Leith Street
CONTRACT VALUE £46 million
SIZE 18,500 square metres

Allan Murray Architects 2001

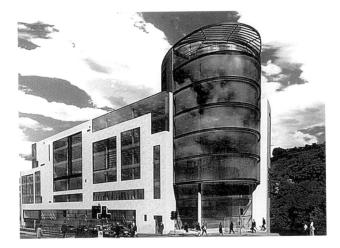

Allan Murray Architects 2001

Pizza Express, Deanhaugh Street

Originally a Georgian villa, the Edinburgh Savings Bank received a baronial makeover by McGibbon & Ross in 1900 and a 1930s extension by William Paterson.

Malcolm Fraser has opened the building up to light and especially to the river, and raised floor and terrace levels to give sightlines over the existing riverside wall. The striking blue cubist extension, replacing the 1930s one, is panelled with American cherry wood and has a tall glass oriel sailing out from the corner, again with a panorama over the river. Under this window a heavy stone-faced column, somewhat reminiscent of the thick corner column of the Palazzo Ducale in Venice, anchors the whole extension and the precarious window and neatly divides the corner door-opening in two.

ADDRESS Deanhaugh Street
CLIENT Pizza Express Ltd
SIZE 305 square metres (3300 square metres)
BUS 28, 29, 80
ACCESS open to public

Malcolm Fraser Architects 1997

New Town

Malcolm Fraser Architects 1997

Broughton Road Housing

This modern corner tenement block isn't actually on the corner. On the street elevation it has a stone façade bordered vertically and horizontally by striking light-blue panelling which makes the corner extra sharp and neat. Cutaway windows emphasise the vertical. The red rendered rear of the building with punched-through windows gives it a mysterious Aldo Rossi light-and-shade effect.

ADDRESS 47 Broughton Road
CLIENT Link Housing Association
CONTRACT VALUE £600,000
BUS 35
ACCESS view from exterior

Percy Thomas Partnership 1998

New Town

Percy Thomas Partnership 1998

Mid-west

Morrison Street Goods Yard Development

The masterplan for this former goods yard, which runs from the Haymarket at the Morrison Street/Dalry Road junction through to the Western Approach Road, won a developer competition. A new link road between Morrison Street and the Western Approach Road has now been established (Morrison Link). This was to be lined with a new hotel development with towers or turrets to emphasise the entranceways (see the Travel Inn with its glass lanterns above roof height, page 9.6), and new housing in a circus and a crescent (see page 9.4) to form the quiet southern edge, continuing the residential atmosphere of Dalry Place.

The edge of the site was to be dominated by offices and retail in continuation of the Dalry Road shopping area, and a five-star hotel in a crescent format would overlook Morrison Street. Neither of these two last stages of the plan have been carried out and the Morrison Street/Dalry Road corner is presently used for car parking.

Masterplan Percy Thomas/Kneale & Russell Architect 1990

Morrison Street Goods Yard Development

Masterplan Percy Thomas/Kneale & Russell Architect 1990

Mid-west

Morrison Circus and Crescent Housing

One of the most misconceived attempts to gain instant *genius loci*, Morrison Circus and Crescent housing is a quick run-off of a pseudo-New Town design. There is neither grandeur nor postmodern irony in the flimsy mock-palace fronts; the geometry is simplistic and thus tyrannical. There is no relationship to landscaping either to the front or rear, and no axis or throughway leading to anything else. In fact the whole circus is so relentless, introverted, and undifferentiated as to make the Stepford wives' housing seem by comparison a vision of authenticity.

Behind the circus a crescent of housing for rent displays a less rigid form and slightly more interesting façades with stone courses through the brick, and postmodern detailing of the heavy cornicing, arched doorways and keystones.

ADDRESS Morrison Circus/Morrison Crescent
CLIENTS Circus, Malcolm Housing Association, Woolwich Homes and Napier University; Crescent, Canmore Housing Association
CONTRACT VALUE Circus, £3.5 million; Crescent £2.75 million
BUS 2, 35
ACCESS view from exterior

Percy Thomas Partnership 1995/1995

Percy Thomas Partnership 1995/1995

Travel Inn

This was the first city centre hotel by the Travel Inn chain. The two phases of the project which join the Western Approach Road to Morrison Street make this hotel Edinburgh's largest in terms of room numbers, with 282. Standard chain specifications for room layout meant that the architects could concentrate on the external appearance of the black pasture sandstone buildings and surrounding hard landscape.

The first phase has fairly traditional siting, massing, form and exterior treatment reflecting those of the other buildings in the nearby New Town. There are also more contemporary elements like the lantern above the stairwells and the glass curtain-walled 'conservatory' to Morrison Street.

The second phase swings away from those traditional streets towards the Western Approach Road and its more modern environment of speed and the machine. This wing is therefore more appropriately minimal and sleek, shorn of cornices, with a stepped plan tapering to a slim, vertically emphasised gable. The pavilions at either end, one of which forms a bridge to phase one with a glass wall framed in French white limestone, and the other in slabs of black granite, emphasise the Jekyll and Hyde effect. Neat 'sculptural' effects on this second wing include the curved steel colonnade on the ground floor echoing the form of the building opposite, the lighting from the fluorescent tubes clad in coloured gels illuminating the balconies through the glass-walled pavilion, and the rooftop lantern reduced here to a single elongated cuboid of clear glass.

ADDRESS Morrison Link
CLIENT Morrison Street Hotel Ltd
ENGINEER Blyth & Blyth
BUS 2, 35
ACCESS open for bookings

Andrew Doolan Architects 1995/1999

Andrew Doolan Architects 1995/1999

Fountain Park

On a site formerly occupied by a brewery, this leisure complex comprises a 12-plex cinema, a fitness club, a tenpin bowling rink, 3D i-WERKS theatre, various bars and eateries and a nightclub. The architects say that the complex was designed 'to present itself to both Dundee Street and the Western Approach Road, with an appropriate scale and architectural response to each'.

The cinema and the iWERKS Theatre providing 2835 seats are set in the north-east corner of the site, sharing foyers and concession units, thus enabling 'cross-over' interest and providing a 'distinguished entrance' and promotional space for the operators.

On the Dundee Street side the complex is organised like a high-tech French courtyard house with a clear hierarchy of functions. The highest pavilion, set furthest back and facing directly out on to the main road, houses the cinemas; the lower wings flanking this part house bars and restaurants to service them. Pedestrians who are not frightened off by the huge gateway pillars can enter by a central covered walkway. The walkway turns out to be only a bridge over the car park, leaving the pedestrian no ground to expect special treatment. The cutaway to the car park reveals it all – this complex was built for, indeed on top of, the motor car.

The façade to the Western Approach Road is utilitarian with the warehouse wall broken up by a series of round stairwells with frosted glass. The main entry to the car park is on this side. The opening of the complex has caused some controversy. The ladies' toilets in the Eros and Elite club contain 'tubicles' – that is a two-WC cubicle supposedly enabling women to fulfill their innate desire to chat with a friend while they both sit on the pan. Meanwhile the men's urinals in the Megabowl are not so social, featuring screens showing TV programmes over which these sporting chaps may relieve themselves.

Hugh Martin Partnership 1999

Hugh Martin Partnership 1999

Fountain Park

Are we to be surprised when the people who gave us these fetishistic and scatological obsessions turn out not to be libertines at all but paranoid schizophrenics? There have been worries, we are told, about security and 'anxiety over packs of troublemakers' (*Evening News*, 24 November 1999) – 56 CCTV cameras are fixed around the complex and nearly 60 private security officers employed.

ADDRESS Dundee Street
CLIENT Scottish and Newcastle Ltd
CONTRACT VALUE £18.5 million; iWERKS, £2.5 million
SIZE 23,200 square metres (250,000 square feet); iWERKS, 2600 square metres (28,000 square feet)
BUS 2, 35
ACCESS open for bookings

Hugh Martin Partnership 1999

Hugh Martin Partnership 1999

Fountain House

A pavilion form with the office space set around a central atrium, Fountain House was designed as an object building to be viewed from all four sides. An effect of light and transparency is gained by the strip windows and metal panels of the main body rising up out of a heavy rubble plinth. This effect is continued by the deep-set clerestorey windows and the over-sailing pavilion roof held up by detached concrete pillars.

ADDRESS 160 Dundee Street
CLIENT Scottish Courage Ltd
CONTRACT VALUE £6.5 million
SIZE 4600 square metres (49,000 square feet)
BUS 1, 2, 28, 34, 35
ACCESS view from exterior

Hugh Martin Partnership 1995

Mid-west

Hugh Martin Partnership 1995

Slateford Green Housing

To have a car or not to have a car, this is the conundrum towards which the whole design of this question-mark-shaped scheme seems to be orientated. Residents have to agree not to keep a car on the premises but they cannot be obliged not to own one. 'We're not saying they can't have cars – that would be stupid. But we have made the whole area a car-free zone', is the cryptic utterance of one of the developers.

Hailed as the way forward for modern city living when the design was first produced, the buildings were no sooner complete than it all came down to earth when the neighbours started to complain. The traffic congestion will now become worse, they claim, because the newcomers with no parking spaces of their own will simply create more demand for the existing ones. Perhaps the situation could be resolved by issuing parking permits, but it does seem that there are elements of petty jealousy in the claims.

The scheme won an international competition to design not only for a car-free environment but also to use energy-efficient and sustainable principles. The 120 flats of two-to-four-storey height enclose a courtyard garden (no vehicles permitted), and the site is skirted by pedestrian and cycle routes.

The elevations are appropriately deep green in colour (sto-acrylic render on a glass-fibre scrim) and the timber-frame construction is from prefabricated panels with ground-floor units rainscreened in cedar boarding. The traditional close-entry system is used for the flats, with stairwells constructed from precast-concrete units with facing masonry. Each stairwell is marked out at roof level by the steel-framed turret clad in aluminium and glass block. The roofing is of aluminium which can be recycled at the end of its useful life.

There are many low-energy features to the design. Warmcel 500 is used

Hackland & Dore 1999

Hackland & Dore 1999

to insulate the walls, and this material also 'breathes' to let moisture out. Conservatories for passive solar heat gain are provided in most flats.

The primary heat source, however, is reject condensate piped from the nearby North British Distillery at low cost. Provision is also made for the fitting of photovoltaic panels to power internal and external lighting.

ADDRESS Slateford Green (off Slateford Road)
CLIENT Canmore Housing
ENGINEER Harley Haddow & Partners
BUS 4, 28, 35, 44, 66
ACCESS view from exterior

Hackland & Dore 1999

Mid-west

Hackland & Dore 1999

Edinburgh Prison Visitors Centre

Essentially a waiting room for prisoners' visitors, this facility provides a café, children's playing areas, storage for personal belongings and baggage, toilets, and meeting, TV and counselling rooms at the entry point to the prison. Funded by a charity and designed in consultation with various bodies including the prisoners' support group and the prison governor, it is staffed by the WVRS (who, of course, do not wear uniforms) and attempts to get away from the institutional and oppressive atmosphere of more traditional prison waiting rooms.

The immediate and literal uplifting point about this building is the striking, prepatinated-copper pitched roof. This roof slopes up towards the prison like the raised triangular lid of some toy box, and thus allows for a tall glazed south-facing façade on this one-storey building. In many ways this is reminiscent of a modern church building, not only in its encouragement of thoughts towards the light and higher things, but even in its very structural quotations – like the heavy laminated curving wooden beams (yellow pine glulam) which soar up and out beyond the walls like those of St Benedict's Church in Drumchapel by Gillespie Kidd & Coia (1967; now demolished).

On the outside the walls are a mix of render and bare calcium-silicate brick (especially on the back of the staff quarters), and the church theme again is evident with a 'ripple effect' of narrow wooden-framed windows curving in and out of the façade to lead the visitor to the entrance by the tower feature. On the inside this ripple effect also has the function of giving a certain privacy to the seating bays arranged along that wall, separated by structural-steel cruciform columns.

Inside the electric doors the visitor is greeted by the timber-panelled reception and the whole space opens along and up in light to the east end. In the tower feature is a further waiting area with a strip window through

Gareth Hoskins Architects 2000

Mid-west

Gareth Hoskins Architects 2000

which those departing can watch for their taxi or driver.

You can only wonder if the brief for this building did not simply hanker for an equally oppressive all-singing-all-dancing 'God is love' evangelistic school of waiting-room design to replace the old 'institutional guilt of sinners and their children's children' school.

On the other hand, there is a great practicality to the design of this building; some 1200 visitors arrive each week, 70 per cent of whom are women – many bringing children – and strict security screening had meant long queues forming outside in all weathers. This facility even provides, aside from the storage for personal belongings, play areas for children both outside and in, baby-change and crèche facilities, food and drink for those who have come far, and a back door to allow for the 'escape of the "girlfriend" when the "wife" and children arrive'.

ADDRESS Saughton
CLIENT The Onward Trust
ENGINEER Ove Arup & Partners
CONTRACT VALUE £800,872
SIZE 468 square metres (5000 square feet)
BUS 3, 25, 26, 27, 28, 33, 34
ACCESS view from exterior

Gareth Hoskins Architects 2000

Mid-west

Gareth Hoskins Architects 2000

Water of Leith Heritage Centre and Walkway

New walkways from town, cantilevered out from the bank of the river, pass under the railway bridge and canal viaduct and come to a courtyard which steps down to the river in front of the old school. This is an important point on the Water of Leith where it crosses the Union Canal, the railway, and the Lanark Road. The extension to the existing building is a timber-clad, concrete-floored strip, which also stretches down towards the river and straddles the walkway with a portal-like feature to give a feeling of 'entrance'. There are also steps up to a viewing platform by the canal, and a 'ford' to help walkers cross the Lanark Road bridge.

ADDRESS Lanark Road, Slateford
ENGINEER White Young Green
LANDSCAPE ARCHITECT Grazyna Portal
SIZE 335 square metres (3600 square feet)
BUS 44, 66
ACCESS open to public

Malcolm Fraser Architects 2000

Mid-west

West

Church Rooms, Colinton Parish Church

The church gardens here are celebrated as the inspiration of Robert Louis Stevenson's *A Child's Garden of Verses*. To the south-east of the grade B-listed sanctuary (Sydney Mitchell, 1908) lie the church rooms, originally built as a stable block but extended several times. The awkward shape, size and layout of these rooms caused some inconvenience.

Page & Park have rebuilt them to a new design incorporating the existing stone walls in a poetic modern composition of a steel-framed cedar-clad building with a monopitch zinc roof and extensive glazing.

The upper level has a kitchen, main hall, foyer, vestry, reception, and disabled-access toilets; on the lower level are the main toilets, another small kitchen and meeting rooms. The foyer on the main floor is now the main entrance to the sanctuary, and thus the 'functional heart' of the building. It is fully glazed and welcoming, and the large timber-surrounded glass doors give a certain moment without pomposity to the entrance. The foyer is spacious and light and encourages the congregation to meet and mingle before and after the services.

Structural steel beams cross the ceiling of the main hall, and the south-east corner with its fixed wooden bench and steel pillar running through the windows is immediately inviting. It is in this corner – also picked out on the façade by its heavy zinc cladding – that the full liberating effect of this building can be experienced, with the full-height glazing to the south providing a panorama of trees and the Water of Leith.

With the smaller windows to the south and south-east giving partial views of the gardens, and the view through the kitchen to the south-west window framing the village roofs heading up the hill, you are encouraged to collect and compose your own image of, and stance to, the world outside. Similarly, looking back to the interior of the building, to the broken corner where the strict rectangle of the main hall opens and flows

Page & Park Architects 1999

Church Rooms, Colinton Parish Church

West

Page & Park Architects 1999

out to the irregularity of the foyer (at least when the sliding panels are open), you may see shafts of sunlight penetrating the rooflights, and beyond that a sandstone corner of the old church itself, and thus you are invited to be aware of, to explore, and to use these interconnecting spaces.

CLIENT Kirk Session, Colinton Parish Church
ENGINEER Oscar Faber
CONTRACT VALUE £529,300
BUS 5, 10, 16, 32, 45, 47, 52
ACCESS open to public

Page & Park Architects 1999

West

Colinton Surgery Extension

Additional community consulting and office spaces were needed for this single-storey building of 1986. Horizontal extensions were built at both ends with a new first floor to the north. A section of the roof and ceiling was removed and replaced by a concrete floor and timber-frame construction, slotting in, piggy-back style, to the existing framework. The double-height large latticed-glazed wall frames the yellow staircase to the first floor.

ADDRESS 296B Colinton Road
CLIENT Dr Chalmers and Partners
BUS 5, 10, 16, 32, 45, 47, 52
ACCESS view from exterior

Gordon & Latimer 1997

Colinton Surgery Extension

West

Gordon & Latimer 1997

Wester Hailes

Built between 1969 and 1975, Wester Hailes was the last in Edinburgh's ring of peripheral estates. Much of the original housing was unpopular and notorious for design and construction faults and in 1988 Wester Hailes was chosen as one of four estates to take part in the regeneration strategy, 'New Life for Urban Scotland'.

There were originally 24 high-rise blocks. Eighteen of them have now been demolished. A locally controlled housing association was set up. Much new housing has been built and the 1970s shopping centre has been refurbished – £66 million has been spent in ten years.

Comprehensive Design Group Ltd (masterplanners) 1997

West

Comprehensive Design Group Ltd (masterplanners) 1997

Multiplex Cinema

This bulky portal steel construction with large corner blocks clad in stone matches the refurbished cladding of the shopping centre to Westburn Place. The double-height glazed entrance, however, faces to the car park at the rear, accessed by stairs up the side of the shopping centre. Eight digital-sound cinemas and a function room give it a floor area of 3252 square metres.

ADDRESS Wester Hailes
CLIENT Highland and Universal Properties Ltd
BUS 3, 28, 32, 33, 52, 58
ACCESS open to public

Comprehensive Design Group Ltd 1997

Comprehensive Design Group Ltd 1997

Community Library

These three linked but separate pavilions whose rotating volumes enclose Westburn Place from the front of the shopping centre, together with the standing fins, centre the bus stop. The library has a steel frame with precast in-situ concrete floors, and the cladding of modular masonry panels blends with both the shopping centre façade and the square. The curved aluminium roofs are exposed internally in the double-height spaces and on the exterior their standing-seam profile handles the step down from the shopping centre to the children's playground and bus stops. The glazed fronts of the library, the stone-paved horizontal, and the standing fins create an intriguing relationship between inside and outside spaces.

ADDRESS Wester Hailes
CLIENT City of Edinburgh Council
SIZE 1400 square metres (15,000 square feet)
BUS 3, 28, 32, 33, 52, 58
ACCESS open to public

Comprehensive Design Group Ltd 1997

Comprehensive Design Group Ltd 1997

Western Avenue Housing

This new housing reflects not only community participation in design, but also the consideration given to positioning windows to gather sunlight and provide surveillance rather than conforming to the 'idea of a geometrically precise masterplan'. The resulting composition is of a pragmatic siting of different forms of housing – single-family dwelling, low rise, etc. – which resembles a 'conventional' pattern of village streets.

There is also wide use of vernacular materials and decoration with a postmodern flavour; round glass-bricked stairtowers capped with candle-snuffer roofs, Fyfestone and rendered façades, high gables, unexpected balconies, quoins, ridgestones and skewputts.

Dumbeg Park by the same architects is also an interesting development if less variegated in its Mackintosh modernist style. I suspect this site with its stricter stylistic consistency will 'age' more quickly.

ADDRESS Western Avenue (Westburn village)
CLIENT Wester Hailes Community Housing Association
ENGINEERS Westburn, Cundall Johnston & Partners; Dumbeg, Rennick Partnership
CONTRACT VALUE Westburn, £5.2 million; Dumbeg, £2.7 million
BUS 28, 33
ACCESS view from exterior

Smith Scott Mullen & Associates 1995/1997

Smith Scott Mullen & Associates 1995/1997

South Gyle and Edinburgh Park

Mid Gogarloch Syke Housing

What a relief it is, here in a sea of phoney stone-faced 'rustic' cottages by Wimpey, to find an island of red-brick houses arranged around an informal square, where each main elevation shows some thoughtful and honest expression of their contents and purpose.

But not only has thought been given to 'dwelling' here, but also to what kind of dwelling is possible. Horizon Housing Association, which organised the competition for this site won by E & F McLachlan in 1995, has a particular interest in developments which include a proportion of wheelchair-standard houses.

Sixteen out of 27 units here are adapted for special needs and 'barrier-free' measures have been used throughout all the units. These measures include: no external steps, all ground-floor units wheelchair accessible, stairways designed as low-pitch single flights, window-sill heights low, and all bathrooms in all units designed to be usable by residents or visitors in wheelchairs.

The scheme has a social focus on the square and the projecting bay with zinc roof is a major element in the design, unifying the nine different house types as well as establishing an interior–exterior link.

ADDRESS Mid Gogarloch Syke, South Gyle
CLIENTS Horizon Housing Association
ENGINEER Brand Leonard Consulting Engineers
BUS 58
ACCESS view from exterior

E & F McLachlan Architects 1996

E & F McLachlan Architects 1996

The Younger Building

The two three-storey 5000-square-metre modules of the building are separated by a glazed entrance hall and linked on the upper levels by open galleries. The plan is symmetrical around this central axis with 13.5-metre-deep floorplates and a central atrium in each module.

The entrance hall is paved in green slate and the suspended ceilings and cladding on the side of the glazed lift shafts are of maple veneer. The Dunhouse sandstone towers containing stairways and service cores and the feature entrance are an attempt to match the stolid castle style of Drummond House next door, also owned by the Royal Bank of Scotland. The glazing modules with the painted steel channels articulating the curtain walling are a wide-eyed yearning for the low-energy credentials of the Edinburgh Park façades (see page 11.6).

This building sits between Edinburgh Park and South Gyle and at best could be said to act as an intermediary between the two; at worst to be ambiguous.

ADDRESS South Gyle
CLIENT RBS Property Developments Ltd
CONTRACT VALUE £14 million
BUS 2, 22, 58A
ACCESS view from exterior

Michael Laird Partnership 1999

The Younger Building

South Gyle and Edinburgh Park

Michael Laird Partnership 1999

Edinburgh Park

'It was obvious by the mid 80s that there was a shortage of modern high-quality offices and factory space in Edinburgh'. So said councillor George Kerevan (*The Scotsman*, 27 November 1992) of the decision by Enterprise Edinburgh Ltd (a company in which he was a leading light and which later became New Edinburgh Ltd (NEL) in partnership with the Miller Group) to develop a business park along a 56-hectare strip of land to the east side of the A720 Edinburgh city bypass. It was to be Scotland's largest commercial venture and Kerevan explained that business was gearing up to move out of Edinburgh city centre anyway, and this development would stop them moving away to locations in Fife or West Lothian.

This area was known then as Redheughs, a name which had first appeared in records around 1400 but one which was clearly not felt to be suitable – perhaps too Scottish in its closing conjunction of consonants – for an international business park. How bizarre then to note that the leader of the council that decided on this change of name signs himself as the orthographically unrepentant Mark Lazarowicz. There was some indecision and for a time the venture went under the geographically inexact title of Maybury Business Park before the present name was fixed.

Naming problems notwithstanding, the councillors went straight to the top for a masterplanner and invited celebrated American modernist architect Richard Meier to do the work. Meier had never built in this country before and it is a matter of embarrassment to NEL that after completion none of the clients chose him to design their building.

The masterplan itself shows the influence of plans for Edinburgh New Town, with the same concern for geometrical layout of urban grids and their relationship with landscaped gardens. Like the original New Town plans, Meier's masterplan also set some standards for the building work. There is a general four-storey height limitation (except for some pivotal

Richard Meier (masterplanner) 1992

Richard Meier (masterplanner) 1992

buildings) and he calls for an expression of energy-conservation design on the façades. The whole site, landscaping and plantings included, is set out on a 4-metre grid. A writer in the RIBA *Journal* (September 1989) claimed that Meier uses the same principles for his urban design as for his individual buildings: 'That is, firstly, that local reference should be sought, distilled, abstracted, and finally reinterpreted; secondly, that a kind of geometric order underpins all design; thirdly, that structure should be modified by concerns for space and time; and fourthly, that rotational and volumetric disjunctions enliven design'.

The masterplan has, however, not been without its critics. One look at it, or a visit to that part already completed, will demonstrate that Meier has swapped what Robert Louis Stevenson called the 'draughty parallelograms' of the New Town for the windswept parking lots of the business estate. The decision to build Edinburgh Park as an 'out of town' development rather than a city centre one has been questioned. It seems to depend too much on the car ('extravagant parking provisions' said *Prospect* in 1993) and as such appears to be out of step with current planning philosophy both in Edinburgh and beyond.

Although it is possible to come to the park by public transport, the likelihood is that any pedestrian would simply be intimidated by the spread of the buildings and the vast car parks. This type of exurb development risks losing both the benefits of urban living and those of the suburbs. Quotes in *The Scotsman* from the staff of the Royal Bank seem to substantiate this problem: 'the thing I miss personally is something like getting a haircut near the office', said one, and 'in the evenings getting out of the industrial [*sic*] estate is hell', said another.

One further criticism is similar to that James Craig received for his New Town plan more than 200 years ago: is the plan too rigid and geomet-

Richard Meier (masterplanner) 1992

Richard Meier (masterplanner) 1992

rical? 'Classicism is fine for cemeteries', as the late Bruno Zevi famously remarked. William Stark criticised Craig's plan for being too formal and not having enough of a relationship with the landscape, and the *National Biographical Dictionary* said it was ' utterly destitute of any inventive ingenuity or any regard for the natural features of the ground'. Do these criticisms also hold for Meier's plan here in the flatter west?

Ian Wall of NEL has worked very closely with Richard Meier and is sure that Edinburgh Park can answer to these criticisms. The next phase of Edinburgh Park to the south towards the railway will not have the same problem of rigorous linear geometry and wide car parks. This phase is completely pedestrian, has a more dense urban feel and includes walkways, an urban square and services. The transport problem ought to be eliminated as a new railway station will open and a guided busway, CERT (City of Edinburgh Rapid Transport), will pass through here on the way to the airport (15 minutes travel time).

Ian Wall is also very careful to stress that the part completed now is wide and open precisely because it is a 'park'. The plantings, the running water and wildlife create a very relaxing atmosphere. £6 million was spent landscaping before the development of offices. Ian White Associates did the design, with three lochans – small inland lochs – in front of the offices. These lochans with 300,000 trees and bushes and ducks, geese, moorhens, etc., were supposed to be formed from the Gogarburn flowing down through the site. Unfortunately nitrates carried in the burn from farming land upstream means that when it settles a thick algae forms. So for the moment tap water is circulated through the lochans and the burn is culverted through the site.

BUS 2, 22, 58A

Richard Meier (masterplanner) 1992

South Gyle and Edinburgh Park

Richard Meier (masterplanner) 1992

Scottish Equitable Building

This was the first building completed at Edinburgh Park, and the largest so far on the site. But as it is situated off to one side behind a huge mound of landscaping, and has rather staid old-fashioned façades of sandstone with long, almost Georgian windows, it does not seem to be a part of the park at all. In fact like some old rectilinear castle on its dun, it turns in on itself with a massive courtyard and rotunda therein. The four-deck car park is the largest in Edinburgh.

CLIENT Scottish Equitable
SIZE 30,000 square metres (323,000 square feet)
ACCESS view from exterior

Koetter Kim Architects 1996

Koetter Kim Architects 1996

Alexander Graham Bell House

The most northerly building acting as a gateway to the Edinburgh Park site as completed by 2000, Bennetts show here their respect and understanding for that principle described above as 'rotational and volumetric disjunctions' which 'enliven design'. An extra lochan (a small inland loch) has been created and a three-storey restaurant, café and boardroom, designed as an eye-catching red cube within a silver cylinder, has been extended out into the water as a landmark feature. The silver of the cylinder is constituted by perforated aluminium louvres and their supports, while the bright, smart style of the café and restaurant extends to genuine Eames and DCW chairs.

The rectangular box of the main building is sectioned by five atriums running across its width. The six floorplates on either side are connected by 'streets' running along the façade overlooking the lochan. In effect there are a number of meeting rooms, break-out and communal areas which allow for creative communication between spaces. Rab Bennetts quotes Kahn's description of the plan as a 'society of rooms'. The exposed in-situ structure of the building is the dominant aspect of the interior and also the basis for thermal stability through passive cooling.

Unfortunately, the main entrance from the car park does seem like the rear of this building rather than the front, but that is a problem for most of these lochanside buildings.

CLIENT BT
ENGINEER Blyth & Blyth
CONTRACT VALUE £18 million
SIZE 14,000 square metres (150,000 square feet)
ACCESS view from exterior

Bennetts Associates 1999

South Gyle and Edinburgh Park

ICL Headquarters

An L-shaped Meier pastiche whose black-tinted windows with feature corners seem particularly closed off to the lochside walk, this 4000-square-metre office block is concrete framed with a white aluminium cladding system.

CLIENT ICL
SIZE 4000 square metres (43,000 square feet)
ACCESS view from exterior

Edmund Kirkby 1994

ICL Headquarters

South Gyle and Edinburgh Park

Edmund Kirkby 1994

John Menzies

John Menzies' headquarters has been in Edinburgh since 1833. By the early 1990s it was clear, they say, that their existing building (a 1930s warehouse conversion) 'was struggling to support the explosion in IT equipment and cabling', vindicating George Kerevan's vision of business needs (see page 11.6). Space was tightly constrained, and staff were flowing into other accommodation. The quality of the space was low, with limited natural light, poor ventilation and long, wide floor areas.

They identified several needs: to convey an image of technical quality to their clients, to find an energy-efficient space, to attract high-calibre staff, and to have a spot away from the city centre but where staff would have 'amenities' and not feel 'captive'. This is where Edinburgh Park and Bennetts Associates come in.

Rab Bennetts describes this building as a 'team player' in the Meier plan, as opposed to a 'landmark' like the BT building (see page 11.14). Nonetheless the building has what *The Architects' Journal* described (30 November 1995) as a 'relaxed assurance and deceptive simplicity'.

Structure is a hybrid of in-situ concrete frame with precast coffered floor slabs, with the concrete exposed throughout. Designed as an open rectangle wrapped around the smaller off-centred rectangle of an atrium, open offices are on three sides of the atrium with meeting rooms and on the ground floor a café/restaurant on the fourth/east side, relating directly through the glass to the waterscape of the park.

CLIENT John Menzies (UK)
ENGINEER Curtins Consulting
ACCESS view from exterior

Bennetts Associates 1994

John Menzies

South Gyle and Edinburgh Park

Bennetts Associates 1994

Scottish Equitable Asset Management Building

Steel framed with a satin anodised-aluminum curtain-walling system, this building is contained within a plinth and two 'book-end' screen walls of Norwegian blue pearl granite. The office organisation is sectioned into two blocks, one twice the size of the other, each with a central atrium. These two blocks are separated by an entrance core which is also marked out in the elevation with walls of the Norwegian granite. This entrance core passes right through the building from front to rear and is Lee Boyd's way of dealing with the problem of car parks at the main entrance and the scenic vista to the rear.

CLIENT (originally) Adobe Systems
ENGINEER Wren & Bell
CONTRACT VALUE £14 million
SIZE 9700 square metres
(104,000 square feet)
ACCESS view from exterior

Lee Boyd Partnership 1999

South Gyle and Edinburgh Park

Lee Boyd Partnership 1999

KSCL Building

This pale, stone-clad building on three levels with black-tinted windows does not seem to respect Meier's wish expressed in the Edinburgh Park masterplan that energy conservation be expressed on the façade. Nor does its strict geometry attempt any communication with the parkland. Planning permission has now been obtained to expand the original L-shaped block to a U-shape with an additional 950 square metres.

CONTRACT VALUE £4.9 million
SIZE 3800 square metres (41,000 square feet)
ACCESS view from exterior

RMJM Scotland Ltd 1997

KSCL Building

South Gyle and Edinburgh Park

RMJM Scotland Ltd 1997

Crammond House

This four-storey white-panelled building with its third-floor terrace leaving the structural frame open in a trellis-work feature is very reminiscent of Richard Meier's modernism. The L-shaped plan is worked out on a 1.5-metre grid and the façades with their integral, perforated, adjustable blinds respect Meier's request to show energy consciousness.

The courtyard enclosed to the rear has a very tranquil ambience induced by the calm of the elevations and the play of the horizontal directionality of the trellis above, the entrance porch roof below and the long stone bench opposite. The effect is heightened by the geometric formality of the planting, two rows of trees and low bushes.

CLIENT New Edinburgh Ltd
CONTRACT VALUE £5 million
SIZE 4536 square metres (49,000 square feet)
ACCESS view from exterior

Reiach & Hall Architects 1999

Crammond House

South Gyle and Edinburgh Park

Reiach & Hall Architects 1999

F1 and F2 Buildings

It is quite confusing to find that the building at the Edinburgh Park address 'F1 [one] site' is occupied by the F1 Group. A steel-framed building, it has a U-shaped plan around a glass-walled atrium which faces the car park. The colonnade on the ground floor in front of the fully glazed restaurant and the terrace on the upper floor constitute the openness to the lochans. To the car-park side is a water feature with a sculpture, *Questor*, by Keith McCarter. Inside the blue panelled curves of the Corbusian-shaped wing to the rear are kitchens, break-out areas, reprographic services, toilets and the fire escape.

The sister F2 building to the south is occupied by the Halifax 'Intelligent Finance' bank. An L-shaped plan around an atrium space facing the car park/entrance, this building has a similar fully glazed ground floor and open upper-floor terrace to the lochans. There are four levels of open/cellular offices on a 7.5 x 12-metre structural grid and the main plant rooms are located on the roof.

CLIENT New Edinburgh Ltd
SIZE F1, 4055 square metres (43,600 square feet); F2, 6700 square metres (72,000 square feet)
ACCESS view from exterior

Parr Partnership 1999 and 2000

Parr Partnership 1999 and 2000

Diageo/UDV Headquarters

According to the architects, this block seeks to 'break away from the repetitive curtain walling which dominates many offices'. The rhythm of solid and void on the façade encourages the eye to try to make sense of it and thus perhaps we have here a real attempt at the expression of energy conservation rather than the usual undying declaration of it. Diageo is the world's biggest drinks manufacturer; is the cantilevered glass cuboid tower which signals the corner of the boardroom a representation of a juice carton? Or is it one of those 'rotational and volumetric disjunctions' by which Meier is said to 'enliven design', and thus does it balance up in its own small way Bennetts' cube and cylinder on the building diagonally opposite, across the lochs?

The steel-framed building has black satin-anodised curtain walling, granite cladding, louvre walls and white render panels. The interior was designed by BDG McColl and Edinburgh-based Skakel & Skakel.

CLIENT New Edinburgh Ltd
CONTRACT VALUE £5.1 million
SIZE 3800 square metres (41,000 square feet)
ACCESS view from exterior

Allan Murray Architects 1999

Diageo/UDV Headquarters

South Gyle and Edinburgh Park

Allan Murray Architects 1999

G2 Building

The z-plan of this building is the architects' response to the brief on this narrow site for an office building which could be subdivided into serviceable units of 28 square metres. The idea of subdivision is already expressed on the façades facing the car park, with glass curtain walling and white rendered slab walls seeming to slide over and dissect one another. The two distinct parts of the building are joined by the bar of the z which is a glazed core entry with a double-height reception, main stair and glazed lift. The feeling here is of dynamism and adaptability.

CLIENT New Edinburgh Ltd
CONTRACT VALUE £2.8 million
SIZE 260 square metres (2800 square feet)
ACCESS view from exterior

Lee Boyd Partnership 1999

Lee Boyd Partnership 1999

G3 Building

Page & Park were asked to produce a building layout that could cater simultaneously for up to 12 tenants. The result is a £5.1 million three-storey L-shaped steel-framed building. The entrance is from the enclosed square and car park to the south; a full-height colonnade wraps around the building. There is a careful, crafted feel with the stained wooden soffits to the open-air arcades, white rendered walls, and the glazed entrance with the open stair climbing inside.

Unfortunately, the outer façades have not had such successful treatment. The curtain walling here has extruded metal mullions which are intended to give a wave-like effect along the building and also to provide some sun shading. The success of the wave effect is debatable, for the mullions give a rather drab grey aspect to these outer walls – how much sun-shading is needed on north- and east-facing walls in Edinburgh?

CLIENT New Edinburgh Ltd
CONTRACT VALUE £5.1 million
ACCESS view from exterior

Page & Park Architects 1999

South Gyle and Edinburgh Park

Page & Park Architects 1999

Lochside Court, British Energy and HSBC Bank Buildings

These two similarly designed but not identical buildings form what the architects call a 'new courtyard grouping'. Originally designed as speculative office blocks, the clients stepped in before work was complete. The larger building has floorspace of 4645 square metres while the other is 2880 square metres, and both have a 15-metre floorplate. Both buildings have gullwing roofs with a deliberate pitch upwards towards the lochans, honey sandstone gable ends, curved entrance features and long top-floor balconies.

SIZE 7525 square metres (81,000 square feet)
ACCESS view from exterior

Building Design Partnership 1995

Lochside Court, British Energy and HSBC Bank Buildings

Building Design Partnership 1995

The Park Centre

Originally earmarked for a building designed by Richard Meier, this site is now occupied by the social focus to Edinburgh Park, designed by the architects who worked with Meier on the masterplan. The building comprises a health club, marketing suite, management offices and a restaurant and bar. A two-storey block with a cylindrical tower emphasising the entrance, the swimming pool has double-height windows overlooking the lochans. This building does not have the austerity of some of the others in the park. It could even be said to be a bit lightweight, and have too much of a bricolage or piecemeal element, with its rotundas, assorted façades, and glazed fronts.

CLIENT New Edinburgh Ltd
CONTRACT VALUE £1.2 million
ACCESS open to public

Campbell & Arnott Architects 1996

South Gyle and Edinburgh Park

Campbell & Arnott Architects 1996

Site A

The most northerly site on Edinburgh Park will feature buildings by Allan Murray Architects, CZWG, and Gordon Murray and Alan Dunlop Architects. The hemispherical A1 site, facing on to the Maybury roundabout, is said by Allan Murray Architects to be the 'most prestigious site' in Edinburgh Park, and will feature an 7400-square-metre office block designed by the masterplanners themselves (originally intended as the British Energy headquarters building – that company has now pulled out). The 'jettied building forms' of CZWG's building will be reminiscent of the Old Town with overhangs and projections from the second floor and roof on the south and west sides to provide sun shading. The new CERT route will pass right through the site.

CLIENT New Edinburgh Ltd
SIZE 7400 square metres (80,000 square feet), plus two other sites totalling 22,300 square metres (240,000 square feet)

Allan Murray Architects (masterplanners) 2000–

Allan Murray Architects (masterplanners) 2000–

North-west

Nursing Home for Young People, Corstorphine Hospital

A residential care centre for young adults with profound learning difficulties and severe physical disabilities, this project and its construction programme were delimited by the fact that Gogarburn Hospital, where the centre was formerly established, was due for closure.

The site, down the east side of the sloping lawns in front of the hospital, has a gradient which makes it most unsuitable for accommodation of wheelchair users. The architect dealt with this problem by creating a stepped row of three ground-level terraced houses with platform lifts between each level. Each house has a communal area on the west side with access to a verandah under the eaves of the wood-panelled gable opening to the lawn. There are six bedrooms and utility rooms – washrooms and treatment rooms – arranged along a central corridor behind this communal room.

The whole complex is organised like a miniature of one side of the High Street herringbone pattern, and thus has a self-contained community ambience with the three main gables facing, chalet-like, on to the lawns and the bedrooms arranged along narrow 'closes' leading back to the road on the east side.

ADDRESS Corstorphine Road
CLIENT Edinburgh Healthcare NHS Trust
BUS 12, 16, 18, 19, 26, 31, 36, 37, 38, 86, 100
ACCESS none

Nursing Home for Young People, Corstorphine Hospital

Archetypes 1999

Edinburgh Zoo Marketing Suite and Picnic Shelter

This bold but dinky little construction is a lesson to architects to be modest in the face of the brief. The zoo wanted a marketing suite but the only vacant piece of land was a small triangular sloping flowerbed behind its main entrance. The nature of this site and budget of around £40,000 necessitated a lightweight construction – timber walls sitting clear of the ground on four concrete-filled drainage pipes.

The building has achieved monumental status nonetheless, with its half barrel roof pointing clerestorey windows towards the entrance building, to the Pentlands beyond and to the sun. A metal bridge with wooden decking connects this hut to the main building, and is supported by one of the retaining walls of the ex-flowerbed.

The exotic shape of the picnic shelter spreads its wings perfectly to cover the parties of schoolchildren who visit the zoo. With hexagonal columns, a steeply pitched rear slope to let the cedar shingles dry out quickly, and an extended bird's-head ridge pole above the front gablet, this small building was put up by trainees from Telford College working alongside the zoo's own works department.

ADDRESS Corstorphine Road
CLIENTS Royal Zoological Society of Scotland and Lothian and Edinburgh Enterprise Ltd
ENGINEERS Phillip Thomson & Partners, Harley Haddow & Partners, Fairhurst & Partners
CONTRACT VALUE marketing suite, £43,000; picnic shelter, £47,000
BUS 12, 16, 18, 19, 26, 31, 36, 37, 38, 86, 100
ACCESS open to public

Smith Scott Mullen & Associates 1997

Edinburgh Zoo Marketing Suite and Picnic Shelter

North-west

Smith Scott Mullen & Associates 1997

Mary Erskine School, Sixth-Form Facilities

An attempt to open up the school to the surrounding parkland that had been given a blank cubist cold-shoulder by Rowan Anderson Kininmonth & Paul's building of 1967, the building is definitely less clean-cut now, less purist but more practical. It provides a sixth-form study area, common room, PE changing facilities, and enables parents and pupils to meet socially at weekends. The sweeping curve of the colonnaded façade and extensive glazed areas behind might form a rent in the fabric of the original tight façade, but it is one that gathers visitors in and also opens out on to the playing fields. The project was funded by an appeal to parents as part of the school's tercentenary in 1995.

ADDRESS Ravelston Dyke
CLIENT the board of governors, Mary Erskine School
BUS 13, 38
ACCESS none

Oberlanders Architects 1995

North-west

Oberlanders Architects 1995

Scottish National Gallery of Modern Art

Lee Boyd have been involved in various projects in this area. They were commissioned to transform the former gymnasium building (built in 1825 by William Burn, converted to a gallery in 1984 by Robert Matthew Johnson-Marshall and Partners) into a visual-arts centre. A new glass and steel entrance with a ramp and a porch roof, and sliding timber-panelled door jazz up the façade and let us know something 'arty' is happening inside.

Inside, a freestanding curved partition behind the reception desk forms a new cloakroom and storage area. New rooflights have been installed and exhibition lighting and new partitions around the walls have created hanging space. For the main gallery Lee Boyd have designed some furniture – the new reception with its sandblasted screen and beech cabinets and menu boards and seating in the basement by the café. A new curved steel and stone-slabbed access ramp to the front portico has been described by the architects as a 'minimalist intervention'.

ADDRESS Belford Road
CLIENT Scottish National Gallery of Modern Art
BUS 13
ACCESS open to public

Lee Boyd Partnership 1989–99

North-west

Lee Boyd Partnership 1989–99

Dean Gallery Conversion

A lottery-funded conversion of the former Dean Orphanage (Thomas Hamilton, 1833) to a gallery housing the Paolozzi collection and other surrealist material. Terry Farrell and Partners have taken a systematic approach, considering everything from the 'doorhandle of the Dean to the landscape'. Indeed, as part of their landscaping project, walkway entrances to the Water of Leith through the cemetery link the gallery with the National Gallery of Modern Art across the road. They are to be specially congratulated for relegating the car to a mere means. By a system of fences, paving, and stairways, they have forced the drivers and passengers once they leave their vehicle to approach the building centrally, obeying 'symmetry' as part of the experience of this building.

Farrell stated as one of their main aims the conversion of the 'drab' interior to match the vigorous and bizarre 'English baroque' exterior. To this end they renounce the clean minimalist design of many modern galleries and claim to have operated under the influence of both the Dadaist principle of juxtaposition and the pile-it-high nineteenth-century approach of John Soane's museum in London.

The ground-floor plan was reorganised and the central corridor spine which passes laterally though the building has been reinstated. Certain details following from these design principles – the *en abîme* effect of having a model of the building itself immediately inside the entranceway; the removed first floor in the room opposite the entrance to give a double-height space under Paolozzi's Cleish Castle ceiling panels; and the transparencies and *trompe l'oeil* effect of windows and light shafts in unexpected places throughout – all heighten the spatial experience of the building.

Unfortunately, despite Farrell's work the experience of this building is neither liberating nor empowering. For Paolozzi pulls out all the

Terry Farrell and Partners 1998

Dean Gallery Conversion

North-west

Terry Farrell and Partners 1998

authoritarian cards in the artist-celeb pack, and his codified obsession with order and authority worked out in a rigid and fragmented geometry only subjects the visitor to his unbearable superego. Anyone who doubts the grounds for such an assertion need only stand under the wee man's big man in the double-height room, or take a look in the café where a huge Paolozzi Newton leans oppressively over a litter of coffee drinkers, sitting daintily (and, it almost seems, fearfully) in the diminutive seats around him.

ADDRESS Belford Road
CLIENTS National Galleries of Scotland, The Dean Gallery, Scottish National Gallery of Modern Art
STRUCTURAL ENGINEER Will Ruud Associates
LANDSCAPE ARCHITECT Ian White Associates
CONTRACT VALUE £6.3 million
BUS 13
ACCESS open to public

Terry Farrell and Partners 1998

Stewart's Melville College Sixth-Form Facilities and Swimming Pool

These two elements wrap around an existing gymnasium and dining block in the grounds of Daniel Stewart's College (David Rhind, 1855). The swimming-pool block has a ski-slope roof rising up to salute the old college, and walls of rendered masonry and glass with one wholly glazed corner. In the interior the steel structure of the roof is exposed, with curved beams crossing the 25-metre pool and a steel colonnade down each side. The freestanding diaphragm walls are used for warm-air ducting.

The sixth-form centre, with the profile of its oversailing monopitch roof, four columns and balcony, gives an elegant stop to the existing dining block.

ADDRESS Queensferry Road
CLIENT Stewart's Melville College
CONTRACT VALUE sixth-form centre,
£650,000; swimming pool, £1.5 million
BUS 40, 41, 43, 47, 55, 82
ACCESS none

Oberlanders Architects 1999

Stewart's Melville College Sixth-Form Facilities and Swimming Pool

North-west

Oberlanders Architects 1999

Maggie's Centre

It was Maggie Jencks' idea to have a centre where those diagnosed with cancer could seek comfort, information, counselling and group sessions in various topics.

Richard Murphy has given this former low grey Victorian stable his trademark treatment with layerings of materials – glass, Douglas fir wood, screens and glass blocks – accent on openings and volumes, colour employed to create a welcoming domestic atmosphere, and the maximum use of space adaptable to both private and public purposes.

The entrance is full of light from both the glass-brick wall and the roof ridgelight. A double stairway with a stepped partition which also serves as a library and leaflet rack leads upstairs to the former hay lofts, now two separate rooms which can be closed off with wooden screens.

Architecturally it's more than appropriate that this little building should sit in behind Womersley's Nuffield Transplantation Surgery Unit. Murphy's therapeutic deconstructivism is not so much an antidote as a welcome complement to Womersley's clinical modernism.

ADDRESS Western General Hospital
CLIENT Maggie Keswick Jencks Cancer Caring Trust
ENGINEER David Narro Associates
CONTRACT VALUE phase 1, £127,000; phase 2, £167,000
BUS 19, 28, 38, 55, 80, 81
ACCESS view from exterior

Richard Murphy Architects 1996

Richard Murphy Architects 1996

Merchiston/Morningside

Technology Building, George Watson's College

A barrel-roofed pavilion with what amount to screen walls wrapped around the glazed façades, inside the emphasis is on openness and clarity. A void opens up to the first-floor balcony, with free-flowing space and exposed pillars and curved trusses supporting the roof.

ADDRESS Colinton Road
CLIENT George Watson's College
CONTRACT VALUE £800,000
BUS 38, 45, 58
ACCESS none

Campbell & Arnott Architects 1994

Technology Building, George Watson's College

Merchiston/Morningside

Campbell & Arnott Architects 1994

Design Studio

Tucked in behind Canaan Lane, the former Morningside Police Station, an 'uninspiring building', has been opened up to light by judicious use of colour, materials, and organisation of space. The drum reception area can be separated from the meeting room by a sliding glass door which creates the feel of a continuous space. Lit at both ends with a glazed door to a landscaped courtyard, and with a workshop area that can cater for eight to ten people, the studio is paper-free. There are no drawing boards; each workstation is fitted with a computer, A1-sized drawer and pedestal unit.

ADDRESS Canaan Lane
BUS 5, 11, 15, 16, 17, 23, 100
ACCESS by appointment

Lee Boyd Partnership 1994

Lee Boyd Partnership 1994

South-east

New Joseph Black Building

A three-storey building whose aluminium cladding and green steel frame give it an appropriately clinical feel. Of the 4425-square-metre floor-space, the lower two levels are multi-role/teaching laboratories and the top level houses research facilities.

The architects say that the form of the building arises directly from the air-movement requirements of the installations which include more than one hundred 2-metre-long fume cabinets. Fresh air is drawn in at the gable and distributed via plenum ceiling and extracted via high-level flues clearly visible on the profile.

The building is joined by an elegant glazed green-framed two-level walkway to the existing chemistry department.

ADDRESS University King's Buildings
CLIENT Director of Estates, University of Edinburgh
CONTRACT VALUE £7.5 million
SIZE 4425 square metres
BUS 38
ACCESS view from exterior

Campbell & Arnott Architects 1999

New Joseph Black Building

South-East

Campbell & Arnott Architects 1999

Royal Infirmary and University of Edinburgh Medical School

A review of healthcare in the Lothians led to the brief for a large specialist purpose-designed major hospital integrated with teaching and research facilities of the medical school replacing the existing Royal Infirmary of Edinburgh and also catering for a transfer of services from the Princess Margaret Rose and City Hospitals.

On a low flat site under the Craigmillar Hill and castle, the curved ladder plan of the main ward block is of modular construction, each module enclosing a courtyard area. This form maximises natural light and ventilation and also provides views from within the building. The curve in the plan also means that no more than a quarter of this massive building is visible from any one position along the façade.

The hospital has 869 beds on three levels. It is 350 metres long and 140 metres wide with a height of 15 metres. The roof is of aluminium and walls are clad with white modular metal panels, with cast-stone feature areas and glazed main entrances.

Patient activity is organised into three distinct categories: in-patients, day cases, and out-patients. The arrangement of clinics, theatres, wards, units and offices is set out accordingly, with, for example, day surgery next to the car parks and public-transport stops, while the reproductive medicine department is at the opposite end of the hospital away from the bustle. The main university building (L-shaped plan and 90-metres long on three floors) has a separate identity and is situated towards the centre of the site linked to the main entrance.

The project has been a focus of some controversy for two main reasons. Firstly, it is said by some to be too far from the centre of town, and that unlike the main institution it replaces it will not be easily accessible by public transport or by car. There are said to be too few parking spaces

Royal Infirmary and University of Edinburgh Medical School

South-East

Keppie Design 2002

– town-planning restrictions are blamed for this restriction.

But surely it would be impossible to find a site for a building this size in central Edinburgh. A juxtaposition of the plan of the hospital on to a plan of Princes Street of the same scale demonstrates just how large the building is. And even if such a huge site could ever be found, the price would be very high – could the NHS afford a commercial price, and would it be worth it?

The other criticisms have focused around the financing of this project by the private financing initiative (PFI). The hospital will cost around £183 million, and a private consortium – Consort, comprising Balfour Beatty, Haden Young, Morrison Construction and Royal Bank of Scotland – will build and run the support services and will rent it back to the NHS for a figure reported as 'around £30 million a year'.

Health Unions and the SNP, among others, oppose PFI because it means the public will pay for but never own the hospital. The architects, however, point out that with PFI they were freed from the normal, tight public capital allowances. More money, they say, could be spent on facilities and quality of finish, for example the external cladding panels, where long-term value for money and reduced maintenance could be proven. The whole building programme is also quicker with PFI and the private sector receives no payment until the hospital is ready for occupation.

ADDRESS Little France
CLIENT Royal Infirmary of Edinburgh and Consort
CONTRACT VALUE £183 million
SIZE 120,000 square metres
BUS 30, 33, 79, 82, 85, 86, 94, 95
ACCESS

Keppie Design 2002

Royal Infirmary and University of Edinburgh Medical School

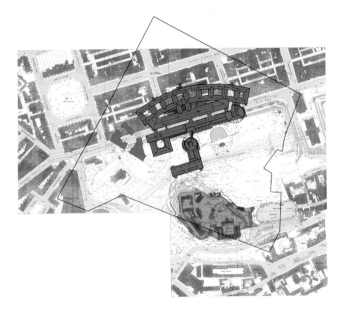

South-East

Keppie Design 2002

Craigmillar Medical Centre

Aside from medical practices, this building includes community facilities, dentists, a crèche, and specialist consulting rooms.

Construction is of load-bearing masonry cavity walls with a partial steel frame supporting open-plan waiting areas. Externally walls are of facing brick with double-height glass-block screens. The standing-seam metal roof is supported on timber trusses and rafters.

Much of Craigmillar has been laid waste by demolition and desolation as it awaits the promised regeneration, but this building does not offer an auspicious start to the programme. It steps back from the main road, seems almost like an overlarge suburban family detached house, and has its single main entrance door hidden under a heavy soffited roof overhang behind a pillar at the top of a narrow set of steps. The architects say that the design 'aims to create a non-institutional building', but is the problem not simply that it is too low-key, but that it is another building which is ashamed of its site?

ADDRESS Niddrie Mains Road
CLIENT Craigmillar Medical
CONTRACT VALUE £1.8 million
BUS 2, 14, 21, 32, 52
ACCESS open to public

Campbell & Arnott Architects 1998

South-East

Campbell & Arnott Architects 1998

Leith and North Edinburgh

Leith and North Edinburgh

The regeneration of Leith started in the 1980s after many of the docks closed down and warehouses – especially those around The Shore – were converted into restaurants, bars and apartments. The regeneration continues on into the new millennium with the siting of the Scottish Office at the Victoria Quay. But the redevelopment is not all for the benefit of well-off or middle-class incomers, for 1500 new jobs will be created at the Ocean Terminal shopping centre, and the 'Brittania' yacht moored outside attracted 500,000 visitors in its first year. Affordable homes for rent are also included in the plans. More than 3000 houses are to be built at the Western Harbour, including high-rise flats, Ocean Heights by Holmes Partnership, and houses on Ronaldson's Wharf by Dignam Read Dewar. Nearly 400 houses will be built in City Quay at Newhaven, and 700 at Granton Harbour. There are also plans to improve transport links by either building a tram route down Leith Walk or extending the CERT route all the way from the airport.

Joppa Pumping Station

This station – pumping station as a sea-going postmodern temple – pumps waste water from Edinburgh's low-lying areas into the two interceptor sewers serving the city. The trussed dual monopitch roof has a po-mo split pediment at the gable and is supported by blue painted-steel colonnades. The pump chambers below are protected by a concrete wave-deflection wall. It is the bevel on this wall and the whole orientation of the pavilion, pointing out to sea, that gives it the nautical feel – all it needs is a couple of banks of oars and the locals would be looking out for Cleopatra and calling it the 'Phryggin' Bireme'.

A pitched-glass-roofed portico leads out to a cobbled forecourt, and a giant concrete rotunda of steps (or seats) leads down to the beach.

ADDRESS Musselburgh Road
CLIENT Lothian Regional Council Department of Water & Drainage
(now East of Scotland Water Board)
BUS 26
ACCESS view from exterior

Lothian Regional Council Department of Property Services 1996

Joppa Pumping Station

Leith and North Edinburgh

Lothian Regional Council Department of Property Services 1996

Coalhill

This project will create a landmark tower to the water's edge, with restaurant and office facilities on the ground and first floors and residential accommodation above.

ADDRESS Leith
CONTRACT VALUE £3 million
BUS 1, 10A, 16, 22, 32, 35, 35A, 52, 88

Allan Murray Architects 2001

Allan Murray Architects 2001

St Ninian's Manse and Quayside Mills

The manse is a seventeenth-century clergy building – now category A-listed – that stood at the head of the first bridge at Leith (demolished late eighteenth century). It has a two-stage lead-covered ogee belfry roof in a distinctive Scots and Dutch form, and crow-stepped gables. Originally a part of North Leith Church, founded in 1493, the church itself stood to the west of the manse on roughly the same outline as the present warehouse. By 1825 the church had been converted into a granary, and until recently it was used by a seed merchant with the manse as offices.

Restoration involved the creation of one office within the manse by Simpson Brown Architects and 19 flats and more office space in the granary by Jim Johnston & Co.

Simpson Brown carried out painstaking archaeological research. Fragments of the original lime coating and limewash colour on the walls were found, and a paint scrape of one of the belfry louvre panels gave an entire history of paint layers since its construction in 1675. The limewash walls and colour of the belfry and louvres have been reinstated, and chimneys built in sandstone according to the form shown in old prints and drawings. The gilded copper weathercock was x-rayed to gain an understanding of its construction and a replica was subsequently made.

Inside, original fire surrounds have been conserved, lime plaster applied to the walls in earlier parts and chestnut lathing to those dating from the eighteenth century. The granary roof structure has been renewed and covered with Scottish slate.

ADDRESS Leith
BUS 10A, 16, 32, 52, 88
ACCESS view from exterior

Simpson Brown Architects/Jim Johnston & Co. 1999

St Ninian's Manse and Quayside Mills

Simpson Brown Architects/Jim Johnston & Co. 1999

Commercial Quay, Renovated Warehouse

In this conversion of a four-storey former bonded warehouse to bars, restaurants, shops, etc., the original fourth floor was removed, and the third-floor level raised, creating greater floor-to-ceiling heights. Along the dockside, facing the Scottish Office, a series of lean-to planar-glazed conservatories have been added, with extruding posts, beams and bracing elements enlivening the façade.

ADDRESS Commercial Street, Leith
CLIENT Forth Ports Ltd in association with The East Old Dock Co.
BUS 10A, 16, 32, 52, 88
ACCESS open to public

Cochrane McGregor Group Ltd 1998

Commercial Quay, Renovated Warehouse

Cochrane McGregor Group Ltd 1998

Leith and North Edinburgh

The Scottish Office

The Scottish Office had decided to rationalise various sites and to get out of its asbestos-ridden New St Andrews House by building a new office in Leith. Like a huge liner sitting in the otherwise empty dock, this new building and its 1500 staff have made quite a contribution to the regeneration of the area. In fact the £37.5 million scheme was announced just before publication of the prospectus for the flotation of the Forth Ports Authority in March 1992 – a 'timely coincidence', commented *The Scotsman* with more than a whiff of cynicism on the sea breeze. Victoria Quay was purchased for £4.6 million and the acquisition of this building follows the principles of the private finance initiative (PFI).

A ladder-plan building with the 'rungs' punctuated by courtyards and four atriums, the building is arranged along the quay and centred on the gap between the Commercial Street warehouses. The clients' concern for security meant that there could only be one, controllable entrance, and this 'drove the fundamental form of the building to a classical format with a central entrance rotunda signalling the building locally'. From this rotunda, a double-height colonnade sweeps out to either side of the building and provides a covered walkway to the car park.

The design pays particular attention to energy efficiency with the atriums providing extra light in the deep plan (15 metres) with triple glazing, interpane blinds, opening windows and high levels of insulation.

Configurations of the floors were kept flexible by the use of movable partitions to divide the space. ESRU of Strathclyde University criticised these arrangements: 'The interior furnishings and fittings, particularly the dark blue partitions, substantially suppress daylight levels. Their removal or replacement would improve daylight distribution'. The joiners, however, must be very happy with these partitions, for they have to be called out – and paid, of course – every time they are moved!

RMJM Scotland Ltd 1995

SCOTTISH EXECUTIVE

Leith and North Edinburgh

RMJM Scotland Ltd 1995

The Scottish Office

Works by more than 30 artists have been acquired and placed throughout the building, including the etched and sandblasted glass screen in the centre rotunda by Tracy McKenna, and in the local meeting rooms there are photographic prints from the archives of the Mitchell Library in Glasgow, and the Royal Museum of Scotland.

ADDRESS Victoria Quay
CLIENT Victoria Quay
CONTRACT VALUE £37.5 million
SIZE 27,800 square metres
BUS 10A, 16, 32, 52, 88
ACCESS view from exterior

RMJM Scotland Ltd 1995

RMJM Scotland Ltd 1995

Ocean Terminal

The three-level mall, a long low building on the eastern side of the Western Harbour, has covered car parking at either end with space for 1500 cars. It also houses department stores, standard retail units, kiosks, restaurants, bars, a health club, a night club, a twelve-screen cinema with a rooftop leisure floor, and a visitor centre for the royal yacht which will be moved alongside.

ADDRESS Western Harbour, Port of Leith
CLIENTS Forth Ports and Bank of Scotland
CONTRACT VALUE £100 million
SIZE 40,800 square metres
BUS 10, 16, 32, 34, 52, 88

Conran & Partners in association with Keppie Design 2001

Conran & Partners in association with Keppie Design 2001

South Fort Street Supported Accommodation

Supported accommodation for ten high-dependency homeless people together with 18 flats on the site of the grade B-listed former Dr Bell's School (James Simpson, 1869) which was refronted as an Italianate villa in 1890. The main body of the existing building is to be refurbished to house communal and staff spaces, while a new wall encloses a private garden with two small 'sub-domestic outhouses' for residents' rooms. In the adjacent grounds, the street frontage will have a contemporary version of the villa stepping up with a curved roof profile to form a high stop to the Pitt Street axis. All supported accommodation is inward facing to the site, while the independent flats look south over Calton Hill and the Old Town above the low warehouses down the rest of the street.

ADDRESS South Fort Street
CLIENT Old Town Housing Association
CONTRACT VALUE main body, £449,000; new build, £966,000
BUS 1, 7, 14, 25A

Ungless and Latimer 2001

South Fort Street Supported Accommodation

Ungless and Latimer 2001

Pitt Street Housing

An interesting take on the tenement, this infill block plays on the Georgian use of railings and bridges over the basement void to the street, and opens up the building with modern use of glazed openings and colour. The stone-faced basement allows for the required density of occupants without having to overshoot the eaves level, and the double-height glazed entry, coloured close walls, and skylight give it a careful and focused touch. Unfortunately the colour of the rendered façade sits quite uneasily with some of its neighbours – it comes from the wrong tradition for this area, especially those Georgians across the street.

ADDRESS 10–26 Pitt Street
CLIENT Port of Leith Housing Association
ENGINEER David Narro Associates
CONTRACT VALUE £1.2 million
BUS 11
ACCESS view from exterior

Lee Boyd Partnership 1998

Leith and North Edinburgh

Lee Boyd Partnership 1998

Public House/Restaurant and Budget Hotel

The question is whether this 60-bedroom hotel with business facilities and a pub restaurant in a New England-harbour style with its gables and timber boarding has the symbolic weight to occupy such a site with such neighbouring features as the fish market, and the heavy stone breakwater. Physical weight was also important during construction as the site is partly on reclaimed harbour land, necessitating extensive pile foundations and the siting of the largest part – the hotel block – on the existing western breakwater.

The roof is of standing-seam aluminium and the timber cladding of weathering cedar. The open colonnade and gables to the south façade echoes the rhythm of the cast-iron and timber bays of its neighbour.

ADDRESS Newhaven Harbour
CLIENT Whitbread Bowland Inns
BUS 7, 11, 16, 25A
ACCESS open to public

Lambie Wright Partnership 1999

Lambie Wright Partnership 1999

Granton Waterfront ('Waterfront Edinburgh')

A masterplan to develop more than 435 acres of the Granton Waterfront over the next 15 years will make it one of the largest brownfield site reclamations in the east of Scotland. The clients have between them raised more than £33 million of public money to clean contaminated sites previously used for oil and gas storage.

The masterplanners envisage a mixed-use development with 5000 new homes, 75,000 square metres of offices, 67,500 square metres of light-industrial space, a marina, ice rink and multi-sports arena, a regeneration of the seventeenth-century Caroline Park, and a university complex. They say that it will be urban rather than suburban with blocks generally of three-storey height coming up to a maximum of six, and involving input from many different architects and landscapers.

Clearly this project will be judged on how it addresses the issues of climate and sustainability, on the rapport it establishes with the existing community (population has halved here since 1951), and how it exploits the waterfront.

CLIENTS Lothian Edinburgh Enterprise Ltd, Scottish Homes, and City of Edinburgh
CONTRACT VALUE £500 million
SIZE 435 acres
BUS 10, 32, 52

Llewelyn Davies (masterplanner)

Granton Waterfront ('Waterfront Edinburgh')

Leith and North Edinburgh

Llewelyn Davies (masterplanner)

Index

Index

Edinburgh: a guide to recent architecture

Index